T P SECRET

SHADY TALES OF SPIES AND SPYING

T P SECRET
SHADY TALES OF SPIES AND SPYING

LONDON, NEW YORK, MELBOURNE, MUNICH, AND DELHI

Senior editor Niki Foreman
Senior art editor Philip Letsu

Project editors Matilda Gollon, Fran Jones, Ashwin Khurana
Designer Hoa Luc

Additional editors Steven Carton, Jenny Finch, Jessamy Wood
U.S. editor John Searcy
Additional design Mik Gates, Katie Knutton, Spencer Holbrook,
Ralph Pitchford, Stefan Podhorodecki, Jane Thomas

Managing editor Linda Esposito
Managing art editor Jim Green
Category publisher Laura Buller

Jacket design Yumiko Tahata
Jacket editor Matilda Gollon
Design development manager Sophia M. Tampakopoulos Turner

Creative retouching Steve Willis
Picture research Harriet Mills

DK picture librarian Lucy Claxton, Emma Shepherd
Production editor Marc Staples
Senior production controller Angela Graef

First published in the United States in 2011 by
DK Publishing, 375 Hudson Street,
New York, New York 10014

Copyright © 2011 Dorling Kindersley Limited

11 12 13 14 15 10 9 8 7 6 5 4 3 2 1
001 – 180643 – Oct/11

A catalog record for this book is
available from the Library of Congress

ISBN: 978-0-7566-8607-9

Color reproduction by MDP, United Kingdom
Printed and bound by LEO, China
**Discover more at
www.dk.com**

T🔑P SECRET

SHADY TALES OF SPIES AND SPYING

Written by:

Laura Buller, Joe Fullman,
Ben Gilliland, and Jim Pipe

In association with

INTERNATIONAL SPY MUSEUM
WASHINGTON DC

Contents

Chapter 3: HOW TO SPY

Chapter 4: CRACKING CODES

Chapter 5:
SPYWARE

Chapter 6:
SHADY HISTORY

Contents

Chapter 7:
SPY WARS

Chapter 8:
SPYING TODAY

FOREWORD

Time: Late Friday. Location: Undisclosed Mediterranean country. Operation: Bug the home office of a Soviet military intelligence officer away on vacation. Easy, right? Well, my two CIA colleagues and I thought so. We slipped in through a window and planted a microphone and transmitter. Now, we just had to conceal the wiring in the basement. After a little digging, the sound of gurgling water caused us to freeze: Our clandestine activity had cracked a pipe! Water was rushing over the floor. We had just 36 hours to fix the leak, cover our tracks, and get out unobserved. Shirts off, we bailed water furiously throughout the night, and thanks to a tech officer trained as a plumber, we did it... but it was a close call.

At the height of the Cold War, the Central Intelligence Agency (CIA) recruited and trained me to run foreign espionage operations. These were the most exciting and challenging years of my life: to live and work under different covers and aliases, to don disguises for

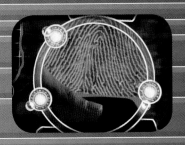

meetings with suspected double agents, to negotiate with a high-ranking terrorist, and even to rig a car to break down on command. Of course, I also had an equal share of report writing, pounding the pavement, and tedious meetings.

Today, at the International Spy Museum, my staff and I work to bring stories like mine and those of other former intelligence officers and spies from around the world out of the shadows and into the light.

As you will see in this book, although the technology has dramatically changed, from ancient times to today spying remains basically the same: Spies everywhere are still searching for the latest and best intelligence. And with this book in hand, you'll know exactly how they do it!

Peter Earnest
Executive Director
International Spy Museum
Washington, D.C.

THE SPY FILES

Why spy, who spies, and what exactly is a spy?
You are about to find out. Welcome to the world
of espionage—a shady, secretive place where
no secret is safe. Spying is all about trying to
uncover secrets, from snooping on the tactics
of a sports rival to uncovering the blueprints
of the hottest technology around. So if you
have a secret, watch out!

Why spy?

To find out secrets, in secret! Spying is carried out by many different people for many different reasons, from governments looking to find out what an enemy country is up to, to companies wanting the lowdown on a rival's latest product. The information they discover, known as intelligence, can then be used to plan ahead.

Government spying

Most spying is done on behalf of countries' governments. They spy on their enemies to see what their military plans are and what weapons they have. They also spy on their allies, to see if they can gain any commercial advantages. They even spy on their own people to try and identify criminals, terrorists, or spies. Spying is big business, with the U.S. government alone spending more than $50 billion a year on intelligence gathering.

Peacetime spying

War isn't the only time a country needs to spy; governments continue to spy on other countries in peacetime in order to stay one step ahead of the game. They look out for potential dangers, such as new weapons or terrorist activity, as well as opportunities, such as the development of new technologies. During the Cold War (1945–1991) between the United States and the Soviet Union, the two sides didn't actually come to blows, but spied on each other intensively throughout.

Wartime spying

Finding out the strengths and weaknesses of an enemy can give a crucial advantage in battle. The first known evidence of military spying dates back to the Battle of Kadesh between the Hittites and the Egyptians in 1274 BCE. Since these early times, governments and armies have employed spies to gather information about their opponents—information such as their location, their numbers, the kinds of weapons they have, and their battle plans.

Pretense

In the murky world of espionage, things are rarely what they seem. Some spies become double agents, pretending to spy for one group but actually spying for another. In one instance in the 1940s, Spanish double agent Juan Pujol Garcia, codenamed GARBO, pretended to be working for the Germans but was, in fact, feeding them false information from the British.

Industrial espionage

Spying isn't just about acquiring military secrets—intelligence is anything that can provide an advantage. Many governments have indulged in industrial espionage over the years, trying to find out commercial and technological secrets of their more advanced rivals in the same way that companies will also spy on each other to try and uncover trade secrets.

Watching the watchers

One of the most important functions of spying is to find out not just what the enemy's secrets are, but what the enemy knows about your secrets. Spies try to feed false information to the enemy to throw them off the scent. This is known as counterespionage.

Public surveillance

Governments don't just watch other governments; governments often spy on their own people. In totalitarian countries, where people have no say in who their leaders are, governments may employ a network of spies to make sure that no one is plotting against them. Spying also takes place in democracies, with governments using spies to detect potential criminals, terrorists, and, of course, other countries' spies.

WHO SPIES?

Most spies spy on behalf of someone else. That might be another person, a company, or a government. They act as go-betweens, gathering secrets from one source and passing them on to another. So, if it's not in their personal interest, why would a person enter the risky world of spying? Experts believe that there are four main reasons why people become spies, which they explain using the acronym "MICE"—Money, Ideology, Compromise, and Ego.

WHO

Intelligence agency

Every government employs an organization, known as an intelligence agency, to do their spying for them. These agencies undertake a range of shady and secretive practices, including stealing secrets, planting false information, and conducting surveillance. Each agency employs a range of people to fulfil an array of roles, from the undercover field agents to the administrative and analysis workers.

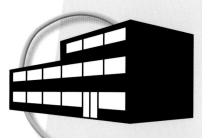

Private company

Alongside government intelligence agencies, many countries also have a network of private intelligence agencies. These agencies are in it for the money, to provide spying services for individual people as well as companies. They are increasingly used by governments, too, to help keep on top of ever-growing amounts of information.

Political group

On the flip side of the coin, governments and companies often get spied on themselves. Political groups (such as peace protesters or environmental activists) who suspect a government or company of doing something illegal or unethical may try to find out sensitive information to make public in the hope that the government or company will change its policies.

Individual

Some people spy without being hired by anybody else. They may happen across some information that they feel could be useful to the government or the wider public, and that they decide to pass on. However, this sort of "walk-in" information is often treated with suspicion by professional spies, since it may not be accurate, depending on the individual's motivation.

Money

Many spies do what they do for the money. For most, it's simply a way of making a living. However, spies who obtain and pass on top-secret information can usually expect to be lavishly rewarded. Aldrich Ames, a CIA agent who secretly spied on the U.S. for the Soviet Union in the 1980s, was paid more than $1.88 million for his information.

Ideology

Some people become spies because of their beliefs. The Cambridge Five, for example, was a group of British spies who passed on secrets from their own government to the Soviet Union in the 1940s because of their Communist beliefs. On the other side of the pond is a similar tale: Ana Montes worked for the U.S. Defense Intelligence Agency starting in 1985 and began spying on her employers on behalf of Cuba because she felt that the United States' policies towards Cuba were unfair.

Compromise

Sometimes people with secrets of their own can be blackmailed into spying. In the 1950s, the West German politician Alfred Frenzel had a secret—he had a criminal record. He hadn't revealed this to the public because he thought he might lose his job. The Czech intelligence agency, the STB, discovered Frenzel's secret and used it to force him to spy for them. Frenzel then lost his job anyway when he was imprisoned for spying in 1960.

Ego

Sometimes spies can be recruited by making them feel good about themselves. It's believed that FBI agent Robert Hanssen began spying for Russia because he wanted to become a glamorous James Bond–style figure. The least common of the four motivations, ego is most likely to motivate a person working in a low-paid, boring job.

SPOT THE SPY

It's no use just looking for the guy in a hat and trench coat—spies come in all shapes and sizes with the outfits to match. They are all out to snatch secrets from people, but different spies have different roles and different ways of snatching! Whatever they're after, however, no spy should stand out from the crowd...

① **Field agents**
Life as a field agent never has a dull moment. From breaking into buildings to steal files or plant bugs, to driving a get-away car or chatting up unsuspecting targets in a bar, these spies will do anything and everything to nab that crucial piece of info.

② **Assassins**
When an enemy agent needs bumping off, the assassin is called in. Sometimes a rifle does the job, but it can pay to be more inventive: The best assassins make murder look like an accident, and, with a bit of poison to help them with their task, a toothpick or umbrella can be surprisingly deadly!

③ **Whistle-blowers**
These spies are ordinary members of the public who can't keep their mouths shut! Often they work in business or government and decide to leak information about their employers' bad practices and expose them to the world.

④ **Double agents**
These two-faced agents pretend to spy on an enemy organization but then get chummy with them. They give away their employer's secrets and pass them false ones. Two separate phones might make working for two agencies less confusing!

⑤ Industrial spies
Jealous of a rival's business success? Send in an industrial spy. Show them the money and they'll hack into databases, copy designs, and plant computer viruses. A sneaky way for you to find out their secrets and sabotage their success! Mwahahaha...

⑥ Defectors
Defectors are agents who turn themselves over to an enemy agency. They may have gotten themselves into trouble and need to leave in a hurry! "Dangles," on the other hand, pretend to defect but are actually handing over false information to confuse the enemy.

⑦ Saboteurs
Mischievous saboteurs undermine the enemy. With a range of tactics up their sleeves, they create chaos in order to change a situation to their side's advantage. Cutting communication lines, damaging property, or blowing up transportation links are all par for the course.

⑧ Surveillance squads
These all-seeing, all-hearing mobile units are equipped with high-tech cameras and listening devices. They wait outside, ready to track the target's every word and move. But it's not all exciting—there's a lot of hanging around between the action. Just try to stay awake...

⑨ Bureau staff
Back at headquarters, the sharpest minds are hard at work. Handlers—the linchpins of any job—are cooking up the field agents' next mission. Analysts make sense of gathered information to see what's going on. The cryptologists, who have a knack for puzzles, crack coded messages and make their own.

⑩ Couriers
Messengers dash between agents and handlers with packages stashed in their briefcases... or backpacks. Students do the job for Israeli agency Mossad and diplomats are also a good bet—their handy immunity from foreign prosecution means that they can't be arrested.

⑪ Undercover cops
Police detectives investigating crime gangs and drug cartels often work like spies. They adopt the look, live the lifestyle, and hang out with criminals for months or even years to gather the information that they need to prosecute them.

⑫ Moles
Intelligence agencies plant moles in enemy organizations to dig deep and ferret out secrets for them. They're not always in a hurry: "Sleepers" wait for years before they are used; often they need to climb the career ladder to access the high-level information.

GARBO: The SAVIOUR of D-DAY!

BORN IN BARCELONA IN 1912, JUAN PUJOL FOUGHT IN THE SPANISH CIVIL WAR BETWEEN THE FASCISTS AND THE SOCIALISTS IN THE 1930S, BUT CLAIMED NEVER TO HAVE FIRED HIS GUN DURING THE CONFLICT. THE WAR GAVE HIM A GREAT HATRED OF FASCISM, WHICH WAS ON THE RISE IN EUROPE.

BAM

IF FASCISM TAKES HOLD ACROSS EUROPE, IT WILL BE A DISASTER!

WHEN WORLD WAR II BROKE OUT IN 1939, PUJOL DECIDED HE HAD TO HELP DEFEAT THE NAZIS. HE TRIED TO OFFER HIS SERVICES AS A SPY TO THE BRITISH AUTHORITIES IN MADRID, BUT HE WAS TURNED AWAY.

BRITISH CONSULATE MADRID

GO AWAY!

BUT YOU DON'T UNDERSTAND—I WANT TO HELP.

PUJOL HAD AN IDEA. HE'D OFFER TO SPY FOR THE GERMANS INSTEAD, AND THEN FEED THEM FALSE INFORMATION. UNLIKE THE BRITISH, THE GERMANS IN MADRID WELCOMED HIM WITH OPEN ARMS. HE WAS TAUGHT SPY SKILLS, AND WAS GIVEN THE CODE NAME ARABEL.

SO YOU VANT TO HELP GERMANY VIN ZE VAR?

NOTHING WOULD GIVE ME GREATER PLEASURE.

PUJOL WAS INSTRUCTED TO TRAVEL TO BRITAIN. ONCE THERE, HE WAS TO BUILD UP A NETWORK OF AGENTS WHO COULD PROVIDE INFORMATION ABOUT BRITAIN'S MILITARY PLANS. HE WAS THEN TO SEND BACK REPORTS, WRITTEN IN INVISIBLE INK, TO THE NAZIS.

VE NEED TO KNOW ZE MILITARY SECRETS OV ZE BRITISH ARMY.

YOU CAN COUNT ON ME!

USE ZIS INK FOR YOUR REPORTS UND YOUR WRITING VILL BE INVISIBLE. ONLY ZE NAZIS VILL BE ABLE TO READ IT.

INSTEAD, PUJOL WENT TO LISBON IN NEUTRAL PORTUGAL. THERE, HE INVENTED A NETWORK OF IMAGINARY BRITISH AGENTS AND SENT FALSE REPORTS ABOUT BRITAIN BACK TO GERMANY. HAVING NEVER BEEN TO BRITAIN, PUJOL USED A GUIDEBOOK AND MAGAZINES TO FIND OUT BASIC INFORMATION TO MAKE HIS REPORTS MORE BELIEVABLE.

WHAT SHALL I WRITE TO FOOL THE NAZIS TODAY?

THE GERMANS NEVER SUSPECTED A THING.

IN 1942, PUJOL FINALLY MADE CONTACT WITH THE BRITISH SECRET SERVICE, MI6, IN LISBON. IMPRESSED WITH HIS WORK, THEY BROUGHT HIM TO LONDON WHERE THEY GAVE HIM A NEW CODE NAME—GARBO—WHICH REFLECTED HOW GOOD AN ACTOR THEY THOUGHT HE WAS, JUST LIKE THE FAMOUS GRETA GARBO. MI6 WANTED PUJOL TO SEND EVEN MORE FALSE REPORTS TO THE GERMANS, SO THEY TEAMED HIM UP WITH A SPANISH-SPEAKING OFFICER, TOMÁS HARRIS.

WELCOME TO LONDON, MR. PUJOL. YOU'VE MADE QUITE A NAME FOR YOURSELF.

I DID WHAT I COULD, MR. HARRIS.

PLEASE, CALL ME TOMMY. WE'RE GOING TO BE WORKING VERY CLOSELY TOGETHER.

PUJOL AND HARRIS WORKED HARD TO CONTINUE DECEIVING THE GERMANS. OVER THE NEXT TWO YEARS, THEY INVENTED 27 FICTIONAL AGENTS, EACH WITH THEIR OWN LIFE STORY. THEY WROTE 315 REPORTS, EVERY ONE FILLED WITH FALSE INFORMATION, AND EVERY ONE BELIEVED BY THE GERMANS.

I MADE THIS AGENT A PIG FARMER.

MAKES SENSE, SINCE IT'S ALL JUST BALONEY!

PUJOL'S MOST IMPORTANT ACT OF DECEPTION TOOK PLACE IN 1944, WHILE THE ALLIES WERE PREPARING FOR THE INVASION OF EUROPE. THE GERMANS KNEW THE INVASION WAS COMING, BUT DID NOT KNOW WHERE IT WOULD TAKE PLACE. PUJOL AND HARRIS'S FALSE REPORTS HELPED CONVINCE THE GERMANS THAT ALLIED TROOPS WOULD LAND AT PAS-DE-CALAIS IN NORTHERN FRANCE.

VE HAVE RELIABLE INFORMATION ZAT ZIS IS WHERE ZE INVASION VILL TAKE PLACE. ZO, VE SHOULD MOVE ZE MAJORITY OF OUR FORCES ZER, IMMEDIATELY!

IN FACT, THE ALLIES INVADED MUCH FARTHER SOUTH, IN NORMANDY. HOWEVER, PUJOL TOLD HIS GERMAN CONTACTS THAT THIS WAS A DIVERSION AND THE "REAL" INVASION WAS STILL TO COME. PUJOL WAS SO WELL TRUSTED THAT THE GERMANS KEPT MANY TROOPS IN PAS-DE-CALAIS WAITING FOR AN INVASION THAT NEVER HAPPENED.

KEEP A LOOKOUT. VE HAVE IT ON ZE BEST AUTHORITY ZAT ZIS IS VER ZE ALLIES VILL LAND.

EVEN WHEN THE "REAL" INVASION DIDN'T TAKE PLACE, THE GERMANS CONTINUED TO TRUST PUJOL'S REPORTS. THEY EVEN GAVE HIM ONE OF THEIR TOP MILITARY AWARDS, THE IRON CROSS. THE BRITISH, WHO HAD MORE REASON TO BE GRATEFUL, ALSO GAVE PUJOL ONE OF THEIR TOP AWARDS— THE MBE. AFTER THE WAR, PUJOL RETIRED FROM SPYING AND MOVED TO VENEZUELA.

WELL DONE!

CONGRATULATIONS, HERR PUJOL.

EDDIE CHAPMAN: Safecracking SPY!

EDDIE CHAPMAN WAS A NOTORIOUS CRIMINAL IN THE LONDON UNDERWORLD OF THE 1930S. HIS SPECIALITY WAS BLOWING UP SAFES USING GELIGNITE OR "JELLY."

CHUCKLE...

TEE HEE!

BOOM

OH, RATS!

'ALLO 'ALLO 'ALLO, WHAT DO WE 'AVE 'ERE?

YOU'RE FINISHED!

DESPITE HIS HUGE CONFIDENCE IN HIS OWN ABILITIES, EDDIE WAS CAUGHT AND SENT TO JAIL ON SEVERAL OCCASIONS.

WHEN WORLD WAR II BROKE OUT, EDDIE WAS IN PRISON ON BRITAIN'S CHANNEL ISLANDS. IN THE SUMMER OF 1940, WITH EDDIE STILL BEHIND BARS, THE GERMANS INVADED THE ISLANDS. EDDIE THOUGHT THE SITUATION COULD BE WORKED TO HIS ADVANTAGE AND OFFERED HIS SERVICES AS A SPY TO THE GERMANS.

THE GERMANS WERE SHORT OF BRITISH SPIES, SO THEY HAPPILY ACCEPTED. THEY TRAINED EDDIE IN VARIOUS SPY SKILLS, INCLUDING USING A RADIO AND SETTING EXPLOSIVES (ALTHOUGH HE WAS PRETTY GOOD AT THAT ALREADY). THEY THEN PARACHUTED HIM INTO BRITAIN WITH INSTRUCTIONS TO COMMIT ACTS OF SABOTAGE.

HOWEVER, ONCE HE HAD LANDED, EDDIE HEADED STRAIGHT TO THE NEAREST POLICE STATION AND ASKED TO SPEAK TO THE INTELLIGENCE SERVICES. DURING A MEETING WITH MI5, HE OFFERED TO BECOME A DOUBLE AGENT, WORKING FOR THE BRITISH AGAINST THE GERMANS. MI5 ACCEPTED, GIVING HIM THE CODE NAME ZIGZAG.

GENTS, I HAVE AN IDEA THAT I THINK YOU'RE GOING TO LIKE...

WHEEEEEEEE!

COR BLIMEY, WORKING FOR THE NAZIS AND NOW US!

LET'S CALL HIM AGENT ZIGZAG!

INTERROGATION ROOM 2

IN ORDER TO MAKE SURE THAT THE GERMANS STILL THOUGHT EDDIE WAS WORKING FOR THEM, MI5 STAGED A FAKE ACT OF SABOTAGE AT ONE OF BRITAIN'S MOST IMPORTANT AIRPORT FACTORIES. THEY COVERED THE SITE IN FAKE BOMB DEBRIS (WHICH LOOKED REAL TO GERMAN SPY PLANES) AND PLANTED FAKE STORIES IN THE BRITISH PRESS. THE DECEPTION WORKED.

EDDIE PERFORMED AN EVEN MORE SIGNIFICANT DECEPTION TOWARD THE END OF THE WAR: WHEN THE GERMANS WERE TARGETING CENTRAL LONDON WITH DEADLY FLYING BOMBS KNOWN AS V-1 ROCKETS, EDDIE SENT BACK FALSE INFORMATION ABOUT WHERE THE BOMBS WERE LANDING, CAUSING THE GERMANS TO CHANGE THEIR AIM SO THAT MANY OF THE BOMBS HIT THE LESS POPULATED AREAS OF SOUTH LONDON AND THE KENT COUNTRYSIDE.

EDDIE DIDN'T JUST DECEIVE THE GERMANS, HOWEVER. DURING THE WAR, HE GOT ENGAGED TO TWO DIFFERENT WOMEN: ONE IN NORWAY (WHICH WAS UNDER NAZI RULE), AND ONE IN BRITAIN. BUT HE EVENTUALLY MARRIED A THIRD WOMAN, WHO HE'D MET IN THE CHANNEL ISLANDS WHEN THE WHOLE ADVENTURE FIRST STARTED! AFTER THE WAR, EDDIE PUBLISHED A MEMOIR OF HIS ADVENTURES AS A DOUBLE AGENT.

THE SABBOTAGE WAS A SUCCESS!

YOU HAVE PERFORMED WELL...

EXPRESS EXPLOSION AT PLANE FACTORY

YOU'RE RIGHT ON TARGET. KEEP AIMING THERE.

NOR WAY!

YOU CAD!

DUMPSTER DIVING

Companies can never be too careful with their data—unscrupulous business rivals and foreign governments are always trying to uncover trade secrets and new technological advances. Industrial espionage is big business, and spies will go to great lengths—hacking into computers, breaking into buildings, bribing employees, and even "Dumpster diving" (rooting through garbage bins)—for that golden nugget of intelligence. Dive in!

SILK SNATCHERS

Before the sixth century, no one in Europe knew how to make silk, so it had to be imported all the way from China at huge expense. In one of the first recorded examples of industrial espionage, the Byzantine emperor Justinian I sent two monks to China to uncover the secret once and for all. The monks discovered that the cloth was made by weaving threads from the aptly named silkworm cocoons… so they smuggled some silkworm eggs out of the country inside hollow bamboo canes. Smooth work.

GLASS ASSASSINS

In the middle ages, the glassware of Venice, Italy, was the envy of the world. Venice's rulers tried very hard to keep the trade secrets from prying eyes: They forced all glassblowers to live on a small island and forbade them, on pain of death, from moving to other countries, with hired assassins under orders to kill any glassblower who tried to leave the island. Eventually, however, some brave souls did escape and spread their knowledge across Europe.

REVENGE IS COSTLY

There are many different reasons why people steal industrial secrets. John Hebel, an employee of American photocopier manufacturer SDMC, did it for revenge. When Hebel lost his job at SDMC in the early 1990s, he went to work for the company's top rival, Duplo. Using his old voice-mail account at SDMC, he gained access to secret information, which he passed on to Duplo. When he was caught, Duplo was forced to pay SDMC $1 million in compensation. That's one way to make an impression on your new boss!

CONCORDE COPIERS

During the Cold War, the Soviet Union sent spies to the West to root out industrial secrets. In the 1960s, Soviet spies stole the plans for the Concorde—a new supersonic plane then being developed by the United Kingdom and France. A Soviet version, the TU-144, was developed, but the spies must have missed some vital information, since several TU-144s crashed and the plane had to be scrapped.

TOP SECRET

BIN THERE, DONE THAT

Hunting through garbage bins may be one of the most unpleasant parts of a spy's job, but the efforts don't go to waste. In 2001, the world's largest shampoo company, Procter & Gamble (P&G), got ahold of information about the new products of its top rival, Unilever, when its spies went through the garbage left outside Unilever's Chicago offices. However, when the dirty deed came to light, P&G ended up paying Unilever around $10 million in compensation.

A STICKY SITUATION

Bribery is a commonly used trick of the industrial-espionage trade. In 1991, the president of a Taiwanese adhesives company was convicted of buying trade secrets from an employee of a rival American firm. Over an eight-year period, he paid the employee $150,000, which was a bargain compared to the $50–60 million it cost the rival company to develop the adhesives.

CHINESE CHIPS

In 2001, two Chinese engineers were arrested in the United States as they boarded a plane bound for China. In their briefcases were hundreds of blueprints for computer chips belonging to American companies that they had been working for. The engineers had stolen the plans to try and boost China's chip technology. When the chips were down, the silicon spies were sentenced to a year in prison!

FIZZ FAKER

In 2006, an employee of Coca-Cola offered to sell the formula of a new soft drink to the company's biggest rival, Pepsi. However, instead of bubbling over with excitement, Pepsi reported the approach to the FBI. The FBI set up a trap, pretending to offer the employee $1.5 million for the secrets, then arresting her when she tried to hand them over.

BE A GOOD SPORT

So how is your favorite sports team going to win the big game? Training hard is one way, but sometimes a little spying can help give the players that extra edge. The world of sports is awash with spies, each with their own game plan for discovering a team's tactics, or getting their hands on the blueprints of the latest equipment. Time to play ball!

Crafty coaches

In the 1960s, football player Lee Grosscup wrote a book describing the crazy things coaches do to find out the opposition's tactics. These included climbing trees to film rival teams' practice sessions, stealing rival coaches' notebooks, and even installing bugging devices in locker rooms.

Secret signals

In football, coaches use hand signals to tell their players what they want them to do. In 2007, the New England Patriots were caught secretly filming the signals being given by the coach of the New York Jets. It proved a costly film—the Patriots were fined $250,000 and the head coach $500,000.

Snooping scouts

Dave Dunbar, a scout for the Melbourne Australian-rules football team, has been accused of being a serial spy, shinning up trees to watch rival teams, renting houses overlooking rival grounds, and even donning a disguise as a construction worker to watch a rival team from a nearby building site.

Fake formulas

In Formula 1 racing, technology is everything. The cars cost millions of dollars to develop and consist of more than 6,000 specially made pieces. In 2007, an employee at Ferrari passed secret technical details to the team's rival, McClaren. When discovered, McClaren was hit with the biggest fine in sports history—a whopping $100 million.

Sneaky sailors

Technology is often the key to success in yachting, so spying is common. In 2008, the Alinghi team accused the rival BMW Oracle team of breaking into their premises and taking photos of their boat. Back in 1982, the American team allegedly employed divers to spy on their Australian competitors underwater.

Base behavior

Baseball rules forbid teams from recording the hand signals given by catchers to pitchers telling them what pitches to throw. But there's no rule against players figuring the signals out for themselves. When this happens, the players may then devise their own secret code, using coughs and whistles, to tell a batter what to expect.

Long lenses

In 2010, the New Zealand rugby team's coach thought he was taking part in a private practice session for a match against Australia. He didn't realize that a photographer was using a long lens to photograph the document he was holding, showing the team's game plan, which was then published in the press.

Spying on your own

Trevor Graham, an athletics coach accused of providing performance-enhancing drugs to athletes, became a double agent when he sent a syringe filled with a then-undetectable steroid, known as "The Clear," to the U.S. Anti-Doping Agency. They developed a test for the drug and caught a lot of cheating athletes.

Are you being watched?

All governments spy on their own people to try and uncover criminals, root out terrorists, and spot spies. Our modern electronic world makes keeping tabs on the public much easier, and intelligence agencies use a whole host of high-tech methods to watch you.

State of suspicion

In democratic countries, there are legal limits on how much a government can spy on its people—there must be a good reason before the authorities can pry into someone's personal life. In undemocratic countries, however, there are no such restrictions. During the Cold War, East Germany used its secret police, the Stasi, to watch over and monitor the population. Anyone suspected of disloyalty was arrested and could be imprisoned or even executed.

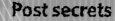

Post secrets

A common method of spying on the public is to monitor people's personal communications. This is known as communications intelligence, or COMINT. In the past, this meant secretly reading letters. In 16th-century England, Elizabeth I's chief spy, Sir Francis Walsingham, opened every letter that left or entered the country. Today, COMINT involves logging phone calls, monitoring web traffic, and reading e-mails and texts.

CCTV

You may think that you're walking around minding your own business, but other people have made it their business to watch you. Closed-circuit television (CCTV) cameras monitor many public places in an effort to prevent crime—but in doing so they keep an eye on us all. Britain is believed to have more CCTV cameras per capita than any other country—up to four million, or one for every 14 people.

Phone tapping

Spies have been secretly listening in to telephone conversations for years. In the early days, a device known as a tap had to be fitted to a telephone line, and the spy had to listen to hours of often-irrelevant conversations. Today, tapping is usually done by computer, and may utilize speech-to-text programs that automatically transcribe everything that's said.

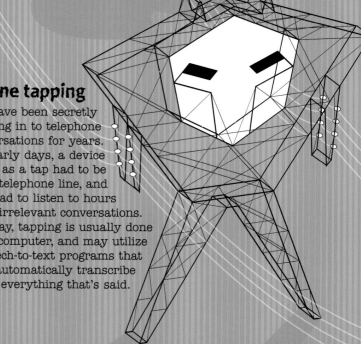

Cell phone tracking

You're not necessarily safe from eavesdropping, even when using a cell phone. A device known as an IMSI catcher can be used to bug your calls, and your phone's signal can be used to pinpoint your location. It's also possible to turn your phone against you: Many police forces have technology that allows them to turn on the internal microphone of a cell phone to secretly listen to conversations—and they can do this even when the phone is switched off!

Biometrics

Governments increasingly keep track of their populations using biometric data—unique physical characteristics, such as fingerprints, eye patterns, facial features, or DNA. Many countries issue passports that hold some sort of biometric information about the holder. The United States collects digital fingerprints and photographs of almost everyone entering the country and compares them against a database to identify known criminals, terrorists, or spies.

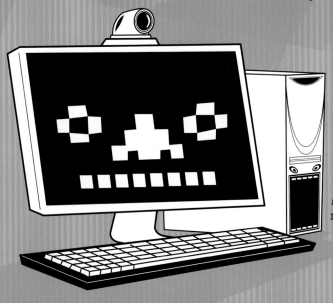

Online surveillance

U.S. intelligence agencies are world leaders at Internet spying, using advanced systems to monitor e-mails and web traffic. These include "packet sniffers"—spying devices that can be attached to Internet networks—and spyware programs, which can secretly log the keystrokes made on a computer. Special software can also analyze messages sent on social-networking sites.

Eyes in the sky

If all this surveillance has got you looking over your shoulder, don't forget to look up as well. Police forces throughout the world use unmanned aerial vehicles (UAVs)—automated aircraft equipped with cameras—for crowd surveillance. In Britain, several police forces operate camera drones, which look like miniature helicopters and hover 49 ft (15 m) above the ground, observing what's going on below. Officers wear special goggles that allow them to see what the drone's cameras see.

TRUE OR FALSE?

In addition to finding out other people's secrets, spying involves keeping your own secrets safe, rooting out enemy spies, and planting false information, or "disinformation." Known as counterintelligence, it's all about lying to the enemy to protect the truth. Read on to discover some historical examples before turning the book over to discover what the real deal was.

The Ramses ruse

In 1274 BCE, Egyptian pharaoh Ramses II heard that the enemy Hittite people had assembled an army and were on the warpath. Ramses marched his army to meet them. When he arrived at the city of Kadesh, he captured two local tribesmen who told him that the Hittite army was still far away. Ramses and his army set up camp, but were suddenly attacked by the Hittites.

Tricking the Ace of Spies

Sidney Reilly was one of the great agents of the early 20th century. Born Georgi Rosenblum in Ukraine, he undertook daring spying missions for Britain during World War I. His dashing exploits earned him the nickname "Ace of Spies." In the 1920s, he traveled to Russia to make contact with "The Trust"—an underground organization dedicated to overthrowing the Soviet Union.

The spy catcher

During World War II, refugees from war-torn Europe flooded into Britain. Anyone suspected of being a spy was interrogated by Oreste Pinto, a Dutch counterintelligence officer who had become Britain's chief spy catcher. Under his questioning, someone with the most convincing story and harmless possessions might still end up being arrested as a spy.

Washington's whitewash

During the winter of 1776, at the start of the American Revolution, the British were confident of victory. John Harrison—a British escapee from an American prison—told the British army at Trenton, New Jersey, that the opposition forces were too weak to attack. So imagine their surprise when American forces marched into Trenton and captured it on December 26!

Operation Mincemeat

In 1943, the body of a British soldier was washed up off the coast of Spain. Handcuffed to the corpse was a briefcase filled with secret British war plans. The information was passed to the Germans, who discovered that the Allies were planning to invade Europe through Greece and Sardinia. The Germans moved many of their forces away from Sicily, where they had previously thought the Allies would invade.

A bodyguard of lies

The Germans were expecting the Allies to invade Europe in 1944, but they didn't know where. However, their spies working inside Britain eventually managed to find out that the Allies would land at Pas-de-Calais in northern France. The Germans prepared by moving the bulk of their troops to Pas-de-Calais where they waited for the Allies to arrive.

The Ramses ruse

This is one of the earliest counterintelligence examples in history. The two tribesmen were... you guessed it, Hittite spies who had deliberately fed false information to the Egyptians. This allowed King Muwatalli II and his Hittite forces to take the Egyptians by surprise. Ramses managed to rally his army, however, and the subsequent Battle of Kadesh eventually ended in a draw.

Washington's whitewash

The British had been fooled by the American commander-in-chief, George Washington. Far from being a loyal British subject, Harrison was actually a double agent. His capture and escape from jail had been staged, and the information he gave the British was false. Washington was a master of counterintelligence and cunningly performed many other deceptions during the war.

Tricking the Ace of Spies

When he got to the Soviet Union, it turned out the ultimate spy had been out-spied; there was no such organization as "The Trust." It had been invented by Felix Dzerzhinsky, the leader of the Cheka, the Soviet Union's counterintelligence agency, to lure Reilly to Russia. Once Reilly was in the country, he was seized by Cheka agents, ruthlessly interrogated, and eventually executed.

Operation Mincemeat

This scheme was one of the most ambitious counterintelligence operations ever. The Allies did plan to invade Sicily but, in order to throw Germany off the scent, they dressed the dead body of a homeless man in a soldier's uniform, gave him a briefcase full of false documents, and set him adrift just off the Spanish shore. The Germans were completely fooled, and the Allied invasion was a success.

The spy catcher

Pinto had a fantastic eye for detail and an almost photographic memory. To Pinto, the more believable a story, the more fishy it was, because spies practiced their stories while innocent people did not. On one occasion he scoured every line of a book that a suspect had in his possession and found that a coded message had been made by using tiny pinpricks under certain letters.

A bodyguard of lies

The invasion actually took place farther south, at Normandy, much to the Germans' surprise. The British had successfully identified every German agent working in Britain, and turned many of them into double agents. These agents fed disinformation back to the Germans as part of Operation Bodyguard, to disguise the Allies' true intentions.

THE DARK SIDE

Welcome to the dark side of spying. Sabotage and assassination are extreme spy tactics intended to deliberately wreak havoc through destructive deeds. From blowing up a weapons factory to shooting a powerful political figure, these devious acts are bloody and brutal. Sometimes committed to prevent further acts of brutality but sometimes not, they show that, in the spy world, things aren't always black-and-white...

BLACK TOM EXPLOSION

In 1916, at the height of World War I, German agents crept into a depot on Black Tom Island, New York, and set fire to ammunition there to keep it from being delivered to their British enemies. This caused a huge explosion, with flying debris puncturing the Statue of Liberty more than a mile (2 km) away.

BOMBING THE BOMB MAKERS

In 1940, the Germans invaded Norway— the site of the world's leading "heavy water" plant. Heavy water is a key material for making nuclear weapons, so the British, worried that the Germans might develop these weapons, parachuted Norwegian saboteurs into the plant. They set off bombs, destroying equipment and the heavy water.

SPECIAL OPERATIONS EXECUTIVE

The agents of the SOE were the sabotage kings of World War II. Founded by the British government, this "secret army" organized many daring sabotage missions and invented ingenious explosive devices, including bombs hidden in lumps of coal, and land mines disguised as cow dung— doubly unlucky for anyone walking on them!

EXPLODING PIPES

By the early 1980s, the United States had become fed up with Soviet spies stealing its secrets and decided to set a trap: The Americans anticipated that the Soviets would try to steal the computer software needed to operate a new pipeline that the Soviets were building, so they booby-trapped the software, causing the pipeline to explode.

JULIUS CAESAR

In 44 BCE, Julius Caesar was the ruler of Rome, but he wasn't loved by all. Some of the senators (Roman politicians) felt that he had too much power and was becoming a tyrant. They lured him to the Senate, where one senator distracted him in conversation while the other senators literally stabbed him in the back.

JEAN-PAUL MARAT

During the French Revolution of the late 18th century, thousands of people were executed in a period known as "The Terror." While powerful politician Jean-Paul Marat lay in his bath, young activist Charlotte Corday stabbed him with a knife that she'd hidden in her clothes, in the hope that it would end the killings... although she herself was guillotined for the act.

FRANZ FERDINAND

Heir to the Austro-Hungarian throne, Archduke Franz Ferdinand was shot by Gavrilo Princip in one of history's most significant assassinations. The Austro-Hungarians blamed Serbia for the killing and declared war. But, with Russia backing Serbia, Germany backing the Austro-Hungarians, and France and Britain supporting Russia, it soon triggered World War I.

ANWAR SADAT

In 1981, during a military parade in Egypt, a group of soldiers stood at attention in front of the president, Anwar Sadat. As Sadat saluted them, one of the troops threw a grenade as the others pulled out guns and shot Sadat, killing him in protest against his signing of a peace deal with Israel.

SPY SECTS

Every country spies, and yet spying is illegal in every country. Spies don't usually spy alone— they operate within a vast and complex global network of spies, watched over by a web of secret services and intelligence agencies. Spying is a dangerous game, and the key to survival is... don't get caught!

THE SPY FACTORY

Unlike James Bond, a real spy can't just set out alone to catch whatever cat-stroking villain might be threatening the world this week. In a real intelligence agency, everyone has defined roles and responsibilities. Some make plans, others collect information, and someone else analyzes it all. A spy is just one cog in the intelligence machine. Welcome to the spy factory.

PLANNING AND DIRECTION

Every factory needs a controller to ensure it's running smoothly and producing top-quality goods. In a country's intelligence agency, a director consults with the government to find out what it hopes to achieve. The director then puts the spy machine to work.

COLLECTION

Following instructions from the director, the spies have to source the factory's raw material, information. Some of it might be available from open sources like "friendly governments" or the Internet. Other pieces are more difficult to find, so field agents are sent to steal data, or technical experts are asked to do some high-tech snooping using spy satellites or phone tapping.

PROCESSING

The raw information needs to be processed into a useful form. It will have come from many different places and been collected in many different ways, so it needs to be translated or decoded into one single format so that it can easily be compared.

INSPECTION

All factories need to be inspected to make sure they're running smoothly and behaving as they should. In democratic countries, intelligence agencies are often inspected by independent figures or bodies who ensure the agency is working in the country's interests and doesn't become too powerful or self-serving.

DISSEMINATION

The brand-new intelligence is now delivered back to the director, who passes it on to the government's policy makers. They can then decide how to react to it. If it's decided that they need more information, the process starts all over again!

ANALYSIS

The spy machine now has a lot of information but not all of it is needed. Analysts examine the information to identify what it means. They then pick out the parts that are important and connect them with other relevant pieces of information to create useful intelligence.

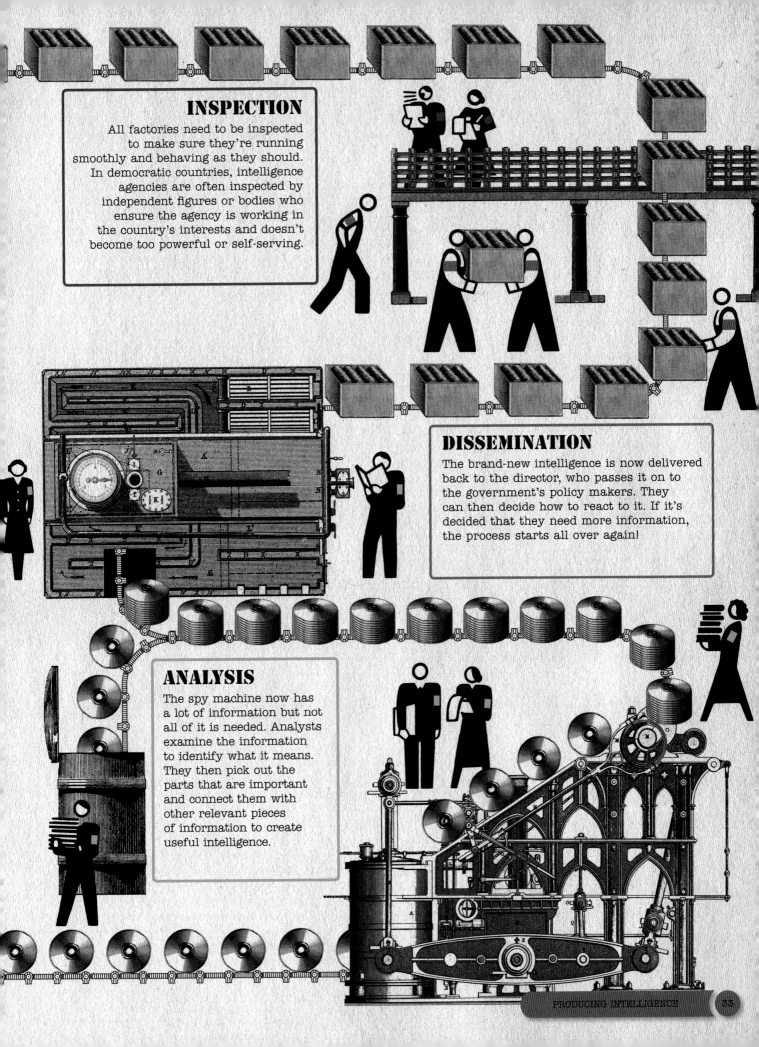

SECRET INTELLIGENCE SERVICE (SIS)

UK

1. Also known as MI6, Britain's foreign intelligence service was founded in 1909. A separate agency, MI5, is in charge of domestic intelligence.

Similar to James Bond's boss, the head of the SIS is known simply as "C," after the first director, Captain Smith-Cumming, who signed all his letters "C."

There is also a real "Q" in charge of gadgets, including wacky devices such as a booby-trapped briefcase and exploding rats.

BUNDESNACHRICHTENDIENST (BND)

GERMANY

1. The BND was originally formed as the FHO (Fremde Heere Ost) during World War II, and was set up to spy on the Soviet Red Army.

After the war, it worked for the CIA, which funded its activities. In 1956, it was taken under the control of the West German Government and renamed the BND.

The agency depends more on wiretapping and electronic surveillance of international communications than it does on field agents.

CENTRAL INTELLIGENCE AGENCY (CIA)

USA

1. The forerunner to the CIA was the Office of Strategic Services (OSS), set up during World War II. It was disbanded after the war but the government set up the CIA in 1947.

The CIA has no power of arrest within the U.S., so it works with the Federal Bureau of Investigation (FBI), a law enforcement agency.

The CIA has invented many devious devices, such as spy planes, satellites, and even a cat bugged with microphones, to spy on its targets.

A WORLD OF SPIES

Almost every country in the world has an intelligence agency. Some countries even have many different agencies that each have their own areas of expertise. They can often have very different goals and may use very different methods, but they all have one thing in common: They are all top secret... some are just a little more secret than others.

GENERAL DIRECTORATE FOR EXTERNAL SECURITY (DGSE)

FRANCE

1. France's current external intelligence agency was formed in 1982 from the many different spy agencies that already existed in France.

Shortly after its formation, the DGSE uncovered a huge Soviet spy network that was stealing secret Western military technology.

But in 1985 it showed lack of judgment when it bombed a fleet of Greenpeace vessels that were protesting against French nuclear testing in the Pacific Ocean.

RUSSIAN FOREIGN INTELLIGENCE (SVR)

RUSSIA

1 The Russian Foreign Intelligence replaced the infamous KGB after the fall of the Soviet Union in 1991. The Russian Federal Security Service (FSB) is responsible for internal security.

The SVR often operates abroad using front organizations. These are legitimate companies used by the agency to hide their spying activities.

One famous front is the Russian airline Aeroflot, which has given a large number of intelligence agents legitimate employment and assisted in agency operations.

MINISTRY OF INTELLIGENCE AND SECURITY (MOIS)
IRAN

? MOIS is Iran's primary intelligence agency and is one of the most secretive in the world; almost nothing is known outside the agency about how it works.

It operates under the direct supervision of its Supreme Leader. It is not accountable to anyone in the government and is not answerable to the country's law.

MOIS is considered to be one of the largest and most active intelligence agencies in the Middle East, and has allegedly masterminded hundreds of acts of terrorism.

MINISTRY OF STATE SECURITY (MSS)

CHINA

The MSS is responsible for both domestic security and foreign espionage. It mainly focuses on stealing weapons technology from the United States.

China has been accused of launching "cyber attacks" on foreign companies and governments, hacking into classified information via the Internet.

Rather than relying only on "official agents," the MSS also uses diplomats, students, and businesspeople to spy on other countries.

AUSTRALIAN SECRET INTELLIGENCE SERVICE (ASIS)
AUSTRALIA

1 ASIS was founded in 1952, but for more than 20 years some members of the Australian Government didn't even know that it existed.

The Australian intelligence agency focuses on gathering information from the local Asia-Pacific region.

In 1983, a training operation held at a hotel in Melbourne went horribly wrong when ASIS agents went too far and actually injured hotel staff.

INSTITUTE FOR INTELLIGENCE AND SPECIAL OPERATIONS (MOSSAD)

ISRAEL

RESEARCH AND ANALYSIS WING (R&AW)

INDIA

1 Mossad was set up to protect the interests of Jews at home and abroad when the modern Jewish State of Israel was formed in 1948.

Jews living around the world can offer to work for Mossad as spies or to provide support to spies. They are called the "Sayanim."

? The location of the agency's headquarters was kept secret until images of the site were shown on Google Earth in 2007, and then published by Israel's largest newspaper.

1 India's external intelligence agency was created in 1968 when the country was at war with China and Pakistan.

The agency acts independently and is not answerable to the Indian parliament in any way.

The R&AW spends most of its time keeping an eye on India's neighbor Pakistan, with which the country has a long history of conflict.

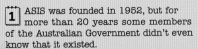
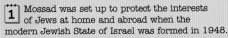

CENTRAL COMMAND

In the past, the location of an intelligence agency's headquarters was a closely guarded secret. Many are still tucked away from prying eyes but, in today's electronic age, when virtual attacks are a real danger, they are more like heavily defended castles than hidden lairs. So what do you need to build the ultimate spy headquarters?

SIS BUILDING, LONDON
Built like a fortress, the so-called "lego" building is shackled with security. Five of its floors are built underground and it even has its own moat.

CIA HEADQUARTERS, VIRGINIA
The CIA headquarters was built with large grounds so that analysts could stroll around undisturbed and think deep thoughts about their cases.

METAL WALLS
Keep secret communications from leaking out by building a copper cage in the walls that blocks radio waves. Add some steel rods and you'll also make the HQ bomb-proof. For a final touch, decorate with bulletproof Kevlar wallpaper.

TRIPLE GLAZING
Disable sneaky bugging devices on the exterior window panes by using triple glazing to keep sound waves from escaping. Also attach white noise devices—they emit a spectrum of sound waves to drown out the sound of speech, foiling those pesky bugs.

CURVED TUNNELS
Sound waves aren't very good at turning corners. So use curved corridors to limit the distance that top-secret conversations can travel around the building.

SECURE CONTROL CENTER
Build a command center with an independent power supply and communication system. Then you can communicate with the outside world even if the rest of the building is attacked or cut off.

HEAVILY GUARDED ENTRANCE
A bomb-proof, snoop-proof building is useless if people can just walk right in! Stop uninvited guests with biometric security and x-ray scanners to check for hidden explosives, weapons, and surveillance devices.

UNDERGROUND SECTION
As any rabbit will tell you: If you want to be safe, burrow underground. By housing your most critical systems and areas below ground, you can protect them from bomb and missile attacks and from electronic surveillance.

SVR BUILDING, MOSCOW
Set in a remote woodland location, the SVR headquarters is also known as "Moscow Center" or just "C."

SIDE BUILDING, BUENOS AIRES
The home of Argentina's secret service is located in downtown Buenos Aires, but curious eyes are kept out by dark, tinted windows.

FORMER DIRECTIA V SECURITATE, BUCHAREST
The bottom of this odd building used to be the Romanian secret-police headquarters. When it was destroyed in 1989, a modern office building was built on top.

AND THE VERDICT IS...

Espionage is a devious world of deceit and duplicity, but is it actually illegal? Unfortunately for a captured spy, the laws that judge spying are just as murky as the spying business and can differ from one place to the next. How spies are treated can depend on where they were caught, what they were doing, and even what kind of clothes they were wearing!

WHAT'S THE CHARGE?

Not many captured spies are actually prosecuted for spying; they are often charged with other crimes instead. This is because it is very difficult to prove that spying has taken place. It is often much easier for a country to prosecute a spy for a different crime. For example, when the United States caught some Russian spies in 2010, they weren't charged with spying but with conspiracy, money laundering, and immigration violations.

ALL COVERED?

Most spies who operate abroad usually report to a "handler" who is usually a government representative the country who is appointed to represent the country abroad). This gives these spies immunity, which means that if they're caught, the worst that can happen is that they will be sent back to their own country and the two countries' governments may exchange a few angry letters. But a spy who doesn't report to an official handler is considered to be an illegal agent and can be prosecuted and imprisoned. Their own government could still come to the rescue, however, by making a deal such as a spy swap.

THE GENEVA CONVENTION

If the enemy caught a spy during the first half of the 20th century, it was legal for them to shoot them then and there. It was brutal but expected, and everyone knew where they stood. This all changed in 1949 following a series of conferences that took place in Geneva, Switzerland, known as the Geneva Convention.

The Geneva Convention attempted to define exactly what a spy was: Article 29 of the Geneva Convention says that a person is considered to be a spy if they are working undercover (or under false pretenses) in enemy territory to obtain secrets that they intend to pass on to that country's enemies.

The Convention also addressed how a captured soldier, or spy, can be treated—an international law to which all countries are supposed to adhere. But the extremity of the punishment, such as the number of years in prison, is then dependent on the laws of the country in which you are caught spying.

DOING TIME

If a spy is actually convicted for espionage, the good news for them is that they're unlikely to be executed because modern international law forbids it. Most countries adhere to this; besides, captured spies are probably more useful alive because they can be interrogated for secrets about their own country. The amount of time they do behind bars, though, depends on where they were caught. In Australia, Canada, and Britain they could be locked away for a life sentence. In Germany or France, they could be free to spy again in just a few years.

IT'S A BIRD, IT'S A PLANE...

What if an intelligence agency decides to use a high-tech aircraft to do some snooping? Sending a spy plane over another country to take some sneaky shots is illegal because, according to international law, it is invading that country's airspace. But intelligence agencies can get around this by using a spy satellite: If the spyware is orbiting in outer space (which isn't owned by anyone), it's not entering anyone's airspace, and thus is entirely legal.

IN UNIFORM OR OUT?

If a spy is caught by the enemy during wartime, they could be let off. If a spy is caught by the enemy during wartime, they could be let off International law states that any spy that is caught while dressed in their own country's military uniform and that is caught while dressed in their own country's military uniform and that is caught as a prisoner of war and cannot be mistreated. But if a spy is wearing undercover and wearing working clothes, or, worse, another civilian clothes, they have much country's uniform and the less legal protection and the enemy can more or less do with them as they please.

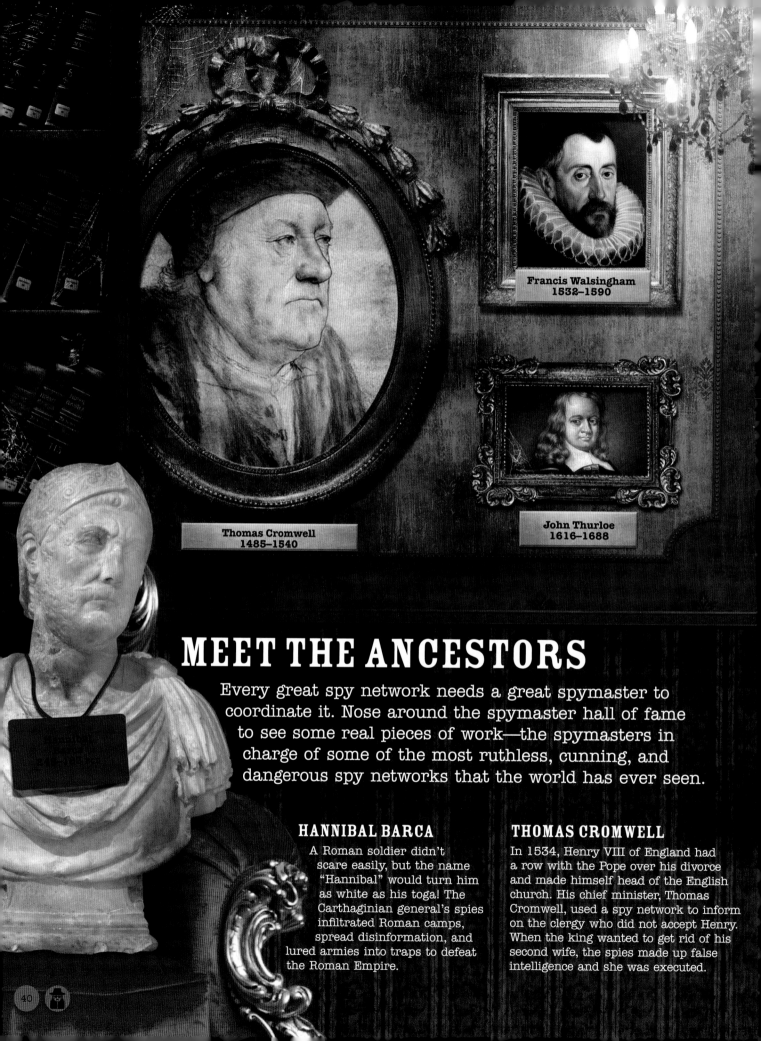

Francis Walsingham
1532–1590

John Thurloe
1616–1688

Thomas Cromwell
1485–1540

MEET THE ANCESTORS

Every great spy network needs a great spymaster to coordinate it. Nose around the spymaster hall of fame to see some real pieces of work—the spymasters in charge of some of the most ruthless, cunning, and dangerous spy networks that the world has ever seen.

HANNIBAL BARCA

A Roman soldier didn't scare easily, but the name "Hannibal" would turn him as white as his toga! The Carthaginian general's spies infiltrated Roman camps, spread disinformation, and lured armies into traps to defeat the Roman Empire.

THOMAS CROMWELL

In 1534, Henry VIII of England had a row with the Pope over his divorce and made himself head of the English church. His chief minister, Thomas Cromwell, used a spy network to inform on the clergy who did not accept Henry. When the king wanted to get rid of his second wife, the spies made up false intelligence and she was executed.

Elizabeth Van Lew
1818–1900

George Washington
1732–1799

Michael Collins
1890–1922

Marcus Wolf
1926–2006

FRANCIS WALSINGHAM

Sworn to protect England's Queen Elizabeth I, Walsingham's spy network covered Europe. In one sneaky setup, his double agents infiltrated an assassination plot by Elizabeth's cousin, Mary, Queen of Scots: They snuck out her secret letters for Francis and, when he had enough proof against her, she was executed.

JOHN THURLOE

In 1649, English political leader Oliver Cromwell overthrew King Charles I. The king's supporters wanted revenge and cooked up plans to assassinate Cromwell. It was John Thurloe's job to stop them. He developed a huge spy network across Europe and took control of the post office, where his spies snooped into suspects' letters.

GEORGE WASHINGTON

Before Washington became the first president of the United States, he was an army general fighting against British rule in America. Taking a leaf out of General Hannibal's book, his spies infiltrated the enemy, reported on troop strengths and movements, and spread disinformation to catch the British off guard.

ELIZABETH VAN LEW

Once the Americans finished fighting the British, they started fighting among themselves. Van Lew was a spymaster during the Civil War between the Union and Confederate armies. She helped Union prisoners escape and gathered details on Confederate troops, which she passed on to the Union commanders.

MICHAEL COLLINS

Collins was an Irish revolutionary leader fighting the British occupation of Northern Ireland from 1919 to 1922. A master of counterintelligence, Collins spied on Britsh spies working against the Irish. His spies were ordinary men and women who infiltrated banks, police forces, railroads, and the postal service.

MARCUS WOLF

The head of East German foreign intelligence for three decades, Wolf was so mysterious that the West didn't even know what he looked like—he was known as "the man without a face." His "Romeo agents" seduced the wives and secretaries of targets in the West German government to get secrets from them.

TRUMPED!

Sometimes one spy just isn't enough. If you want to collect a lot of top secret information from a large area, why not round up a spy ring? In this pack of spy rings, members have infiltrated enemy governments, troops, and intelligence agencies to trump their opponents.

Ethel Gee

Harry Houghton

THE PORTLAND RING

When: ....
Where: 1950s–1961
For who: ....England
Members: ....Soviet Union
Caught or not: 5
....Caught

Two members of this group worked at a naval base in Portland, England, where the British were building their first nuclear submarine. The spies passed information about the project to their ringleader, Gordon Lonsdale, who passed it on to two others in London to send to the Soviet Union, using a powerful radio hidden in their attic.

SPY RINGS

Guy Burgess

John Cairncross

Kim Philby

Donald Maclean

Anthony Blunt

THE CAMBRIDGE FIVE

When: 1930s–1950s
Where: ....England
For who: ....Soviet Union
Members: 5
Caught or not: ....Caught

The Soviet Union wanted spies inside the British government, so it went to England's top university, Cambridge, to recruit five students. The men went on to get top jobs in British intelligence and government and passed secrets to the KGB until they were found out. The identity of the fifth member was unknown until the 1980s.

University of Oslo

THE NILI RING

When: ....
Where: 1917
For who: ....Palestine
Members: ....Britain
Caught or not: ....20+
....Caught

This group of local Jews helped the British prepare for an attack on Ottoman territory during World War I, hoping that a British victory would help the Jews establish their own state. Using carrier pigeons, they reported on weather conditions, enemy troop movements, water sources, and desert routes.

THE XU RING

When: 1940–1945
Where: ....Norway
For who: ....Allied powers
Members: ....Around 1,500
Caught or not: ....Not caught

This huge ring recruited many of its original members from the University of Oslo but later used agents spread all over Europe. From Nazi-occupied Norway, the group used a special courier system to send information about German fortifications and forces back to England. These details proved vital for Allied bombing raids and operations.

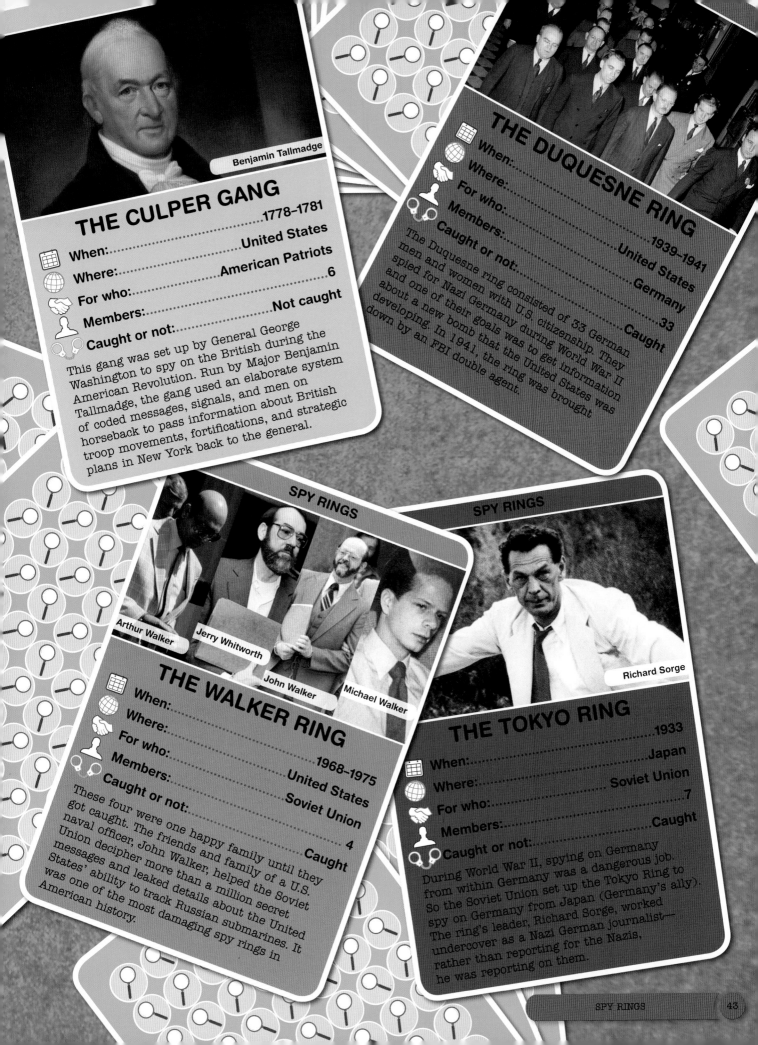

THE CULPER GANG

Benjamin Tallmadge

- 🗓 **When:** 1778–1781
- 🌐 **Where:** United States
- 🤝 **For who:** American Patriots
- 🧍 **Members:** 6
- 🔗 **Caught or not:** Not caught

This gang was set up by General George Washington to spy on the British during the American Revolution. Run by Major Benjamin Tallmadge, the gang used an elaborate system of coded messages, signals, and men on horseback to pass information about British troop movements, fortifications, and strategic plans in New York back to the general.

THE DUQUESNE RING

- 🗓 **When:** 1939–1941
- 🌐 **Where:** United States
- 🤝 **For who:** Germany
- 🧍 **Members:** 33
- 🔗 **Caught or not:** Caught

The Duquesne ring consisted of 33 German men and women with U.S. citizenship. They spied for Nazi Germany during World War II and one of their goals was to get information about a new bomb that the United States was developing. In 1941, the ring was brought down by an FBI double agent.

SPY RINGS

THE WALKER RING

Arthur Walker
Jerry Whitworth
John Walker
Michael Walker

- 🗓 **When:** 1968–1975
- 🌐 **Where:** United States
- 🤝 **For who:** Soviet Union
- 🧍 **Members:** 4
- 🔗 **Caught or not:** Caught

These four were one happy family until they got caught. The friends and family of a U.S. naval officer, John Walker, helped the Soviet Union decipher more than a million secret messages and leaked details about the United States' ability to track Russian submarines. It was one of the most damaging spy rings in American history.

SPY RINGS

THE TOKYO RING

Richard Sorge

- 🗓 **When:** 1933
- 🌐 **Where:** Japan
- 🤝 **For who:** Soviet Union
- 🧍 **Members:** 7
- 🔗 **Caught or not:** Caught

During World War II, spying on Germany from within Germany was a dangerous job. So the Soviet Union set up the Tokyo Ring to spy on Germany from Japan (Germany's ally). The ring's leader, Richard Sorge, worked undercover as a Nazi German journalist— rather than reporting for the Nazis, he was reporting on them.

THE CULPER GANG

IT'S 1778 AND THE AMERICANS ARE REVOLTING AGAINST BRITISH RULE. THE BRITISH OCCUPY NEW YORK CITY AND THE AMERICAN GENERAL GEORGE WASHINGTON NEEDS INFORMATION ABOUT BRITAIN'S POSITIONS AND TACTICS...

AN AMBITIOUS YOUNG OFFICER NAMED BENJAMIN TALLMADGE IS GIVEN THE JOB OF FINDING A SOLUTION.

WE DESPERATELY NEED TO KNOW WHAT THE BRITISH ARE PLANNING!

I KNOW JUST THE PEOPLE TO DO IT...

TALLMADGE'S FIRST RECRUIT IS ROBERT TOWNSEND. AS A WELL-CONNECTED NEW YORK MERCHANT, TOWNSEND HAS GOOD REASON TO BE IN THE CITY AND, AS A LOCAL JOURNALIST, HE HAS GOOD REASON TO BE TALKING TO PEOPLE.

YOUR CODE NAME WILL BE "SAMUEL CULPER, JR."

THE NEXT RECRUIT IS THE SON OF A LOCAL JUDGE AND SOMEONE WHO TALLMADGE ALREADY KNOWS: ABRAHAM WOODHULL HAD SERVED BRIEFLY IN THE LOCAL MILITIA, BUT IS NOW A FARMER.

YOUR CODE NAME WILL BE "SAMUEL CULPER."

NEXT UP IS AUSTIN ROE, A DEPENDABLE LOCAL TAVERN KEEPER. ROE'S COVER STORY WHEN TRAVELING TO NEW YORK WILL BE THAT HE IS BUYING SUPPLIES FOR HIS TAVERN.

YOU WILL BE KNOWN AS "AGENT 724."

THE LEAST RESPECTABLE RECRUIT IS CALEB BREWSTER. HE SERVES WITH THE LOCAL MILITIA AND HAS DEVELOPED A FEARSOME REPUTATION AS ONE OF THE MANY "WHALEBOAT RAIDERS" WHO ATTACK BRITISH SHIPS IN LONG ISLAND SOUND.

YOU WILL BE "AGENT 725."

TALLMADGE'S LAST RECRUIT IS PERHAPS THE MOST UNLIKELY. ANNA SMITH STRONG IS ONE OF TALLMADGE'S RELATIVES. SHE IS VERY WEALTHY AND IS A MEMBER OF THE LOCAL ELITE. HER HUSBAND IS A LAWYER WHO WAS ARRESTED BY THE BRITISH AND LOCKED UP ON BOARD A PRISON SHIP.

YOUR CODENAME WILL BE "NANCY SMITH."

THAT'S JUST FINE... BUT HANDS OFF MY DRAWERS, SIR!

SO TALLMADGE HAD GATHERED TOGETHER HIS SPIES. THEIR IDENTITIES WERE A CLOSELY GUARDED SECRET. EVEN GEORGE WASHINGTON WAS ONLY EVER TO KNOW THEM BY THEIR CODE NAMES! THEY WERE TO BECOME KNOWN AS "THE CULPER GANG."

OK GUYS. YOU KNOW THE DEAL. WASHINGTON NEEDS EYES AND EARS INSIDE NEW YORK...

YOU WILL BE THOSE EYES AND EARS!

THIS IS HOW THINGS ARE GOING TO WORK... NOW, PAY ATTENTION, IT'S VERY COMPLICATED...

"TOWNSEND, YOU HAVE MORE FREEDOM TO MOVE AROUND THE TOWN THAN ANY OF US. USE THAT FREEDOM TO LISTEN IN ON WHAT THE BRITS ARE PLANNING AND USE YOUR COVER AS A JOURNALIST TO QUESTION ANYONE WHO MIGHT BE IN THE KNOW."

I HEAR THEY'RE BRINGING IN A LOAD OF THOSE FANCY NEW CANNONS NEXT WEEK...

HMM, I JUST WISH THEY'D GET US SOME MORE TEA! I CAN'T STAND THAT COFFEE STUFF THEY DRINK AROUND HERE.

"ROE, YOU WILL VISIT ROBERT AT HIS STORE UNDER THE PRETENSE OF BUYING SUPPLIES FOR YOUR TAVERN. HIDDEN IN YOUR 'GROCERY LIST' WILL BE A NOTE FROM JOHN BOLTON (THAT'S MY CODE NAME BY THE WAY) REQUESTING INFORMATION."

THANK YOU, SIR. I SHALL PUT YOUR ORDER TOGETHER SHORTLY.

I HOPE THEY HAVE SOME TEA.

"ROBERT, YOU WILL CLOSE UP YOUR STORE AND HEAD TO YOUR ROOMS. READ THE NOTE AND ANSWER ACCORDINGLY. NOW, YOU MUST HIDE THE NOTE IN SOME GROCERIES... DON'T PACK ANY TEA, THOUGH— IF THOSE BRITS SO MUCH AS SMELL THAT STUFF, THEY'LL CONFISCATE IT FOR SURE. PASS THE PACKAGE TO MR ROE."

HEY! WHAT ABOUT MY TEA?!

"RIGHT, THIS IS WHERE IT GETS DANGEROUS. AUSTIN, YOU WILL NOW RIDE AS FAST AS YOU CAN BACK TO YOUR TAVERN IN SETAUKET. BE CAREFUL, THOUGH. EVERY INCH OF THOSE 55 MILES IS CRAWLING WITH BRITISH RAIDING PARTIES AND BANDS OF HUNGRY BANDITS."

I DON'T SUPPOSE THERE'S ANY CHANCE OF A REST STOP?

"BEFORE YOU REACH YOUR TAVERN, YOU WILL STOP AT ABRAHAM'S FARM. BESIDE THE ROAD, SEVEN PACES EAST OF THE WAY MARKER, IS A LARGE ROCK. BENEATH THAT ROCK YOU WILL FIND A SMALL BOX. PUT THE MESSAGE IN THE BOX AND RETURN TO YOUR FARM."

"ABRAHAM WOODHULL, THIS IS YOUR CHANCE TO TRY OUT THAT NEW SECRET CODE YOU'VE BEEN WORKING ON! ENCRYPT THE MESSAGE AND... OOOH... TELL YOU WHAT, WHY DON'T YOU WRITE IT OUT USING INVISIBLE INK? GALLIC ACID WILL DO THE JOB NICELY!"

INVISIBLE INK... HMM... BLAST IT, WHERE DID I GET TO? I CAN'T SEE A THING!

"IN THE MEANTIME, CALEB, YOU WILL BE SAILING ACROSS THE SOUND IN THAT WHALER OF YOURS. FIND A NICE SAFE COVE AWAY FROM PRYING EYES TO HIDE IN. THEN GET WORD OF YOUR LOCATION TO ANNA."

SHH... DID YOU HEAR SOMETHING? SOUNDED LIKE SOMEONE SPLASHING.

SORRY, I KNOCKED MY TEA OVER.

"ANNA, NOW IT'S YOUR TURN. WHEN YOU GET WORD OF WHERE ON YOUR FAMILY'S LAND CALEB IS HIDDEN, HANG THE APPROPRIATE NUMBER OF BLACK PETTICOATS ON YOUR CLOTHESLINE–HANG TWO IF HE'S IN THE EAST COVE, THREE IF HE'S IN THE WEST COVE... YOU GET THE IDEA."

IS THERE ANOTHER ONE TO HANG UP THERE?

YES, BUT SHE INSISTED WE ONLY HANG UP THREE. CHANGES HER MIND EVERY DAY... STRANGE WOMAN.

"ABRAHAM, YOU WILL BE KEEPING AN EYE ON ANNA'S LAUNDRY. WHEN YOU SEE THE SIGNAL, WAIT UNTIL IT'S DARK AND SNEAK OVER TO WHERE CALEB IS HIDING AND PASS HIM THE CODED MESSAGE."

WHAT DO YOU SUPPOSE HE'S LOOKING FOR?

PROBABLY A DECENT CUP OF TEA!

"CALEB, UNDER COVER OF DARKNESS, YOU WILL ROW ACROSS THE SOUND. BUT WATCH OUT FOR BRITISH PATROLS! IF THEY SPOT YOU, MAKE SURE YOU 'LOSE' THE MESSAGE OVERBOARD. IF ALL GOES WELL, I WILL BE WAITING FOR YOU ON THE OTHER SIDE."

"JUST BECAUSE WE ARE OUT OF BRITISH TERRITORY DOESN'T MEAN WE CAN RELAX. WE HAVE POSITIONED MOUNTED SOLDIERS WITH FRESH HORSES EVERY 15 MILES. I WILL TAKE THE MESSAGE TO THE FIRST RIDER, THEN IT WILL BE PASSED ON TO THE NEXT... AND SO ON. IT WILL REACH GENERAL WASHINGTON IN NO TIME."

"WITH ANY LUCK, THE MESSAGE WILL REACH GENERAL WASHINGTON'S HEADQUARTERS IN NEWBURGH IN LESS THAN A DAY. THE GENERAL, WHO WILL BE IN POSSESSION OF A CODEBOOK, CAN THEN DECIPHER ABRAHAM'S MESSAGE."

AHH... SPLENDID! LOOKS LIKE ANOTHER MESSAGE FROM THOSE CULPER BOYS.

"ONCE THE GENERAL HAS READ THE MESSAGE, HE WILL WRITE US A NEW REQUEST (ENCODED, OBVIOUSLY). HE WILL PASS THIS BACK TO THE RIDER AND THE PROCESS WILL BE REVERSED. CALEB WILL CARRY IT ACROSS THE SOUND, ANNE WILL SIGNAL HIS ARRIVAL, ABRAHAM WILL PASS IT TO AUSTIN ROE, WHO WILL GIVE IT TO TOWNSEND..."

...ANY QUESTIONS?

WHAT WAS THE MIDDLE PART AGAIN?

THE CULPER GANG'S METHODS WERE VERY EFFECTIVE. EVEN THOUGH THEY TOOK PART IN MANY RISKY ENDEAVORS, ASSISTING GENERAL GEORGE WASHINGTON AND THE CONTINENTAL ARMY THROUGHOUT THE REVOLUTIONARY WAR, NONE OF THE MEMBERS WERE EVER CAUGHT BY THE BRITISH.

COVERT CONNECTIONS

Intelligence agencies don't always operate alone to achieve their aims; often they need to cooperate with agencies from other countries to get their hands on the information, or people, that they're looking for. Sometimes they work with "friends," but at other times they are forced to negotiate with the enemy.

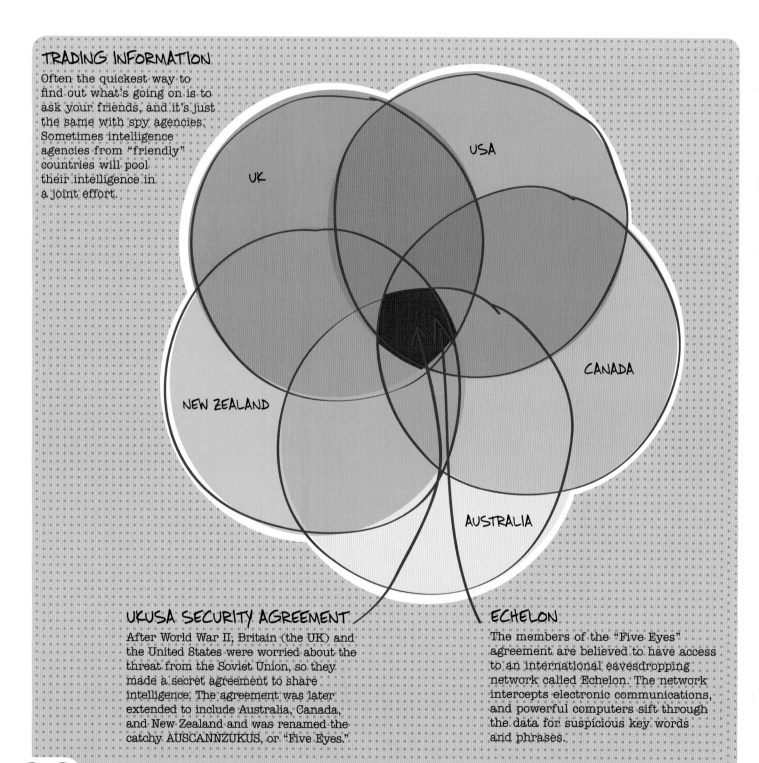

TRADING INFORMATION

Often the quickest way to find out what's going on is to ask your friends, and it's just the same with spy agencies. Sometimes intelligence agencies from "friendly" countries will pool their intelligence in a joint effort.

UK

USA

CANADA

NEW ZEALAND

AUSTRALIA

UKUSA SECURITY AGREEMENT

After World War II, Britain (the UK) and the United States were worried about the threat from the Soviet Union, so they made a secret agreement to share intelligence. The agreement was later extended to include Australia, Canada, and New Zealand and was renamed the catchy AUSCANNZUKUS, or "Five Eyes."

ECHELON

The members of the "Five Eyes" agreement are believed to have access to an international eavesdropping network called Echelon. The network intercepts electronic communications, and powerful computers sift through the data for suspicious key words and phrases.

TRADING CAPTIVE SPIES

Oh no! One of your country's spies has been caught in the act and captured by the enemy—provided you're not going to deny their existence, sometimes the only way to get them back is to make a trade. Hopefully the enemy hasn't gotten too much information out of them yet.

In 1960, an American U-2 spy plane was shot down over the Soviet Union (USSR) and the pilot, Gary Powers, was captured by the Soviets. The United States had also captured a Soviet spy, Rudolf Abel, five years earlier, so the countries made a secret trade in 1962.

In 1964, British businessman Greville Maynard Wynne was accused of spying for Britain and the United States in the Soviet Union. He was exchanged for Konon Trofimovich Molody, a Soviet army officer who had been held in Britain for spying since 1961.

Toward the end of the Cold War in 1985, 29 spies changed hands in the biggest spy swap since World War II. Four spies caught in the West were swapped for 25 held in the East. The swap included a Polish spy convicted in the United States, some West German spies caught in East Germany, and a Bulgarian spy. The Soviet Union was closely involved in the negotiations.

In 1976, the imprisoned leader of Chile's Communist party, Luis Corvalau, was taken in by the Communist Soviet Union in exchange for an imprisoned Soviet human rights activist named Vladimir Bukovsky, who was released to the West.

In 2010, Russia, the United States, and Britain orchestrated a spy swap in which 10 Russian sleeper agents, who had been arrested in the U.S., were deported back to Russia in exchange for four Russians who had been spying for the U.S. or the UK.

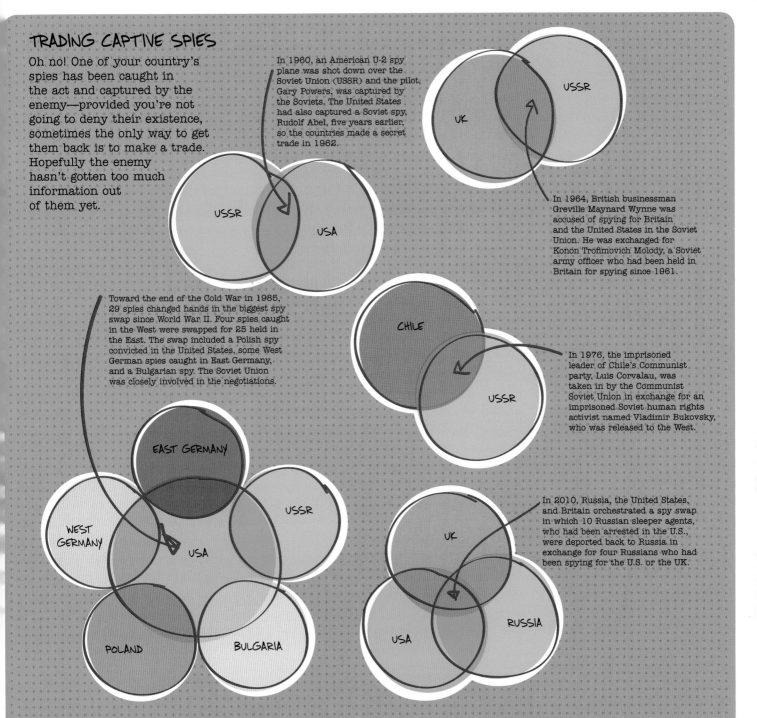

TRADING CAPTIVES

Someone you want to question is on the run in a foreign country. That country might be persuaded to help you get your hands on the suspect by arresting them on your behalf and handing them over. This type of cooperation is known as "rendition," meaning "handing over."

Fighting terrorism
In the past, some suspects have then been flown to a completely different, neutral country for questioning. This is called "extraordinary rendition" and is sometimes used by intelligence agencies in their effort to fight global terrorism. Allegedly, suspects have been moved from where they were arrested to countries with more relaxed human rights laws, where more force can be used to extract information.

TUNING IN

The Cold War was a war of ideas and how better to broadcast ideas than on the radio? Radio Free Europe and Radio Liberty were CIA-funded stations that transmitted news and stories into the Soviet Union and Eastern Europe. But the Communist authorities tried to stop their citizens from listening by using radio-jamming techniques.

IMPOSTER MAIL

During a propaganda campaign dubbed "Operation Cornflakes" in World War II, the Allies bombed German mail trains and hid letters containing anti-Nazi propaganda in the wreckage. The German postal service didn't notice the fakes and delivered them all over Germany with the morning mail.

MORNING NEWS

Propaganda is a crafty tactic that is used to get people on your side. It is the spreading of information to convince others that a certain idea is right, or that another idea is wrong. It has been used since mankind's earliest history and it can take many different forms—from newspaper articles to imagery on the television and the Internet, we are exposed to propaganda from the minute we get up in the morning. It isn't always obvious, and history's sneakiest propagandists have used such cunningly subtle methods that people failed to wake up to the truth.

PLAYING GOD

Roman emperors often saw themselves as gods and preferred it when their subjects thought the same. To encourage this, emperors stamped their portraits onto coins, or commisioned statues of themselves in godlike poses. That way, everyone in the empire knew who was boss.

IMAGE IS POWER

In the 16th century, women were seen as weak and inferior to men. So Queen Elizabeth I carefully crafted her image to ensure that she projected an aura of power. One of her tactics was to pose for portraits that used symbols from ancient mythology, like the phoenix and the serpent, which suggested strength and endurance.

FIGHTING WITH FICTION

During World War I, the British government hired the best authors, artists, and publishers to create propaganda designed to increase support for the war at home. Millions of posters, pamphlets, and short stories depicted shocking atrocities committed by German soldiers, increasing the British public's hatred toward Germans.

DICTATING OPINION

In the 1930s, future dictator Adolf Hitler used propaganda to help his Nazi party take power in Germany. The Nazis set up their own newspapers and only published stories that supported their causes. They also used movies, the school curriculum, and the radio to help influence the opinions and behavior of the German people.

FALSELY ACCUSED

American patriot Benjamin Franklin tried to persuade German troops serving the British to desert them during the American Revolution. He wrote a letter pretending to be from a German prince that exposed supposed British human rights violations. When the letter was circulated, many Germans left their posts.

CHANGING THE CHANNEL

Television and the Internet are now the most powerful tools to influence public opinion. And it's not just advertising companies trying to sell products: During the Iraq War that began in 2003, the CIA and MI6 were accused of leaking news stories to the press to help increase public support for the war in the United States and Britain.

BEHIND THE BARBED WIRE

Tucked away from view in the middle of the desert, on remote islands, or even deep underground, are the very best brains, put to work by their governments to develop the most advanced technology and weaponry in the world. But wherever there's a closely guarded secret, there's a spy waiting to access all areas and uncover it...

KAPUSTIN YAR
Astrakhan Oblast, Russia

When the Soviets defeated Germany in World War II, they captured a number of German V-2 rockets, the world's first rocket-powered missiles and the precursors to all modern space rockets. The Soviets tested and refined the V-2s at Kapustin Yar to develop their own rockets. Apparently, British intelligence guessed that something was going on and sent several spy planes to check it out... but they deny doing so.

SITE Y-12
Los Alamos Test Lab, New Mexico

Welcome to the home of the Manhattan Project, where the world's first nuclear bomb was made in the 1940s. Used to test more nuclear weapons following its initial success story, the base's location was totally secret and security was incredibly tight. But that didn't stop some crafty Soviet spies who managed to infiltrate the project during the 1940s and send valuable nuclear secrets back to Moscow, helping speed along the development of their own nuclear bomb.

NEGEV NUCLEAR RESEARCH CENTER
Dimona, Israel

Israel's nuclear weapons program is based in the Negev Desert, not far from Dimona. The heavily defended facility is hidden deep underground and its airspace is closed to all aircraft. In 1986, a former employee revealed many of its secrets to the British press and he was hunted down by Mossad, Israel's intelligence agency, and imprisoned.

ANTHRAX TEST SITE
Gruinard Island, Scotland

You won't want to vacation on this isolated Scottish island. In 1942, British intelligence heard that Germany was developing biological weapons. British scientists hastily built their own deadly anthrax bombs and tested them at Gruinard. The island was contaminated for 50 years... and the "intelligence" turned out to be false!

AREA 51

Southern Nevada

Contrary to conspiracy theorists, Area 51 probably doesn't have an alien hidden in the basement, but the site really does exist. Hidden deep in the Nevada desert and surrounded by mountains, this is home to the U.S. military's top secret experimental aircraft program, and some of the stealthiest spy planes have been tested here. So no, that's not a UFO—it's just a plane.

DISCOVERER PROGRAM

Palo Alto, California

While the Soviet Union and the United States were publicly trying to build better rockets in the 1960s, both countries were secretly building the first spy satellites. The CIA's satellite program, code-named Corona, was designed and built as a super top-secret, or "deep black," program at a helicopter factory in California. To avoid suspicion, the CIA concocted the cover story that it was simply part of a research program called Discoverer.

YAMANTAU MOUNTAIN

Russia

This top secret complex is so secret that its purpose remains a mystery even today. Intelligence agencies in the West apparently uncovered signs of massive excavations and mysterious entrances, but they won't reveal all their findings. Rumors suggest that the complex was built as an underground command bunker for the Soviet leadership in the event of a nuclear war.

DARPA HQ

Virginia

DARPA (Defense Advanced Research Projects Agency) is a real-life version of Q's laboratory in the James Bond films. The agency builds the gadgets and equipment that make spying possible; therefore much of what they do is top secret. Over the years, they have designed robot spy insects, spy planes that are almost invisible to radar, and software that predicts future terrorist attacks.

HOW TO SPY

So you want to be a secret agent? Discover the skills and experience you need to become a spy. Learn how to dress, use your charm, construct a cover, make dead drops, avoid surveillance, and what to do if you get caught. With the tricks of the trade at your fingertips, you'll soon be walking the walk and talking the talk...

Testing your strength

If you are chosen for an interview, you can expect a battery of tests. Your oral and written communication skills, problem-solving strategies, analytical abilities, and organizational skills will all be put to the test. Examiners will assess how streetwise you are, as well as your overall intelligence and your ability to cope with stress.

Apply yourself

In the past, the various agencies around the world approached the people that they thought were suitable for spying. Today, agencies may also post ads for new recruits. In many countries, you can even apply to be a spy online. What do you need to apply? There are basic age and citizenship criteria and you will need lots of patience since the process can take many months.

Speak another language

Mastering at least one other language and speaking it like a native is a great asset. The languages that are in highest demand often mirror the world's political trouble spots. In 2011, for example, the CIA was eager to recruit Arabic, Chinese, Dari, Indonesian, Korean, Pashto, Persian, Russian, Turkish, Kurdish, and Urdu speakers.

Be outstanding

A candidate should have excellent grades and be the best and brightest in their chosen field. Most espionage agency staffers work as analysts, scientists, and in technology- and language-based jobs. If administration's your thing, there are the same supporting staff roles as in any large company.

The right stuff

The agency will be on the lookout for special personal qualities that set you apart from the rest. You will need to show excellent strength of character, honesty, loyalty, and integrity, and agencies will investigate evidence for all of this in your past with thorough background and reference checks.

Know when to keep quiet

If you want to work at an intelligence agency, you will need extremely high levels of tact and discretion. Gossips need not apply. In many cases, you will be asked not to talk with anyone about your job application. If you get hired, you will be expected to keep quiet about your work, even with your friends and family.

Be prepared to travel

Many spies are required to live or spend some time in a different country. In the CIA, for example, many operations officers spend more than half of their working lives living overseas to collect and handle foreign intelligence. This requires these agents to have a sound sense of independence and adaptability, enabling them to work and live in a foreign place and culture.

Be upstanding

While trouble with the law, or in your school or employment history, isn't ideal, agencies realize that no one is perfect. They will evaluate the risks and benefits of each applicant, but anything in your past that shows personal weakness, or that could leave you open to blackmail or bribery from an enemy, would put you at a big disadvantage.

Be a people person

For certain jobs, you'll need to be a people person with the ability to communicate well and easily socialize. Taking an interest in what makes people tick as well as in world events in general is a definite advantage for a would-be spy.

Be a team player

You'll need to be a trustworthy team player. Intelligence officers can't talk to other people about their work, so there is often an especially strong team spirit. This is a major reason why, when a spy defects to help another country as a double agent, for example, it is such a deeply felt shock to their spy colleagues.

SUPER SPY

You're bright, flexible, and quick-witted—nothing puzzles you for long. You've got guts as well as good grades. You're honest, trustworthy, and a team player. You're ready and willing to serve and protect your fellow citizens. Put all these pieces together and you're the ideal candidate with everything a government agency's looking for in a spy.

MEET THE TEAM

When James Bond leaps into action, he's a one-man army. In reality, however, every operation needs an experienced operations officer or "chief" to run the show, with a team of experts to give the agents the support and protection they need.

Stakeout team

Stale burgers and cold coffee go hand in hand with this boring job. It's all about watching and waiting. And waiting. It can get a little cramped sitting in a car, so it's best to find a room overlooking the target with views of all the exits.

Break-in technician

Top-notch tools and nimble fingers are needed to pick locks, cut through doors, and deactivate alarm systems. Dressing as a handyman is a good way to go unnoticed.

Surveillance

These guys really know how to bug you. They place tracking devices on cars and set up listening devices in rooms as well as on people (in which case the devices are called "wires"). Charisma and a daring sense of fashion are not required—they need to blend into a crowd, and leave no traces behind for the enemy to find.

In the field

Daring yet cool-headed, this field agent is the link between a mole and the chief. These two have set up a meeting by a bus stop— a clever, unsuspicious meet point out in public. The agent checks around to see if their cover is blown. All clear? Yes! He watches for the agreed signals before making contact with the mole.

Garbage expert

It's a dirty job, but someone's got to do it. You'd be amazed what you can find rooting around in someone's garbage: correspondence, phone bills, bank statements, even love letters! Take a peek at the clothesline while you're there to check if they live alone.

Behind enemy lines

A mole may spend years working with the enemy, passing top secret information to the field agent when he can. It's best if a mole doesn't break cover, so any meets take place away from closed-circuit cameras and prying telephoto lenses.

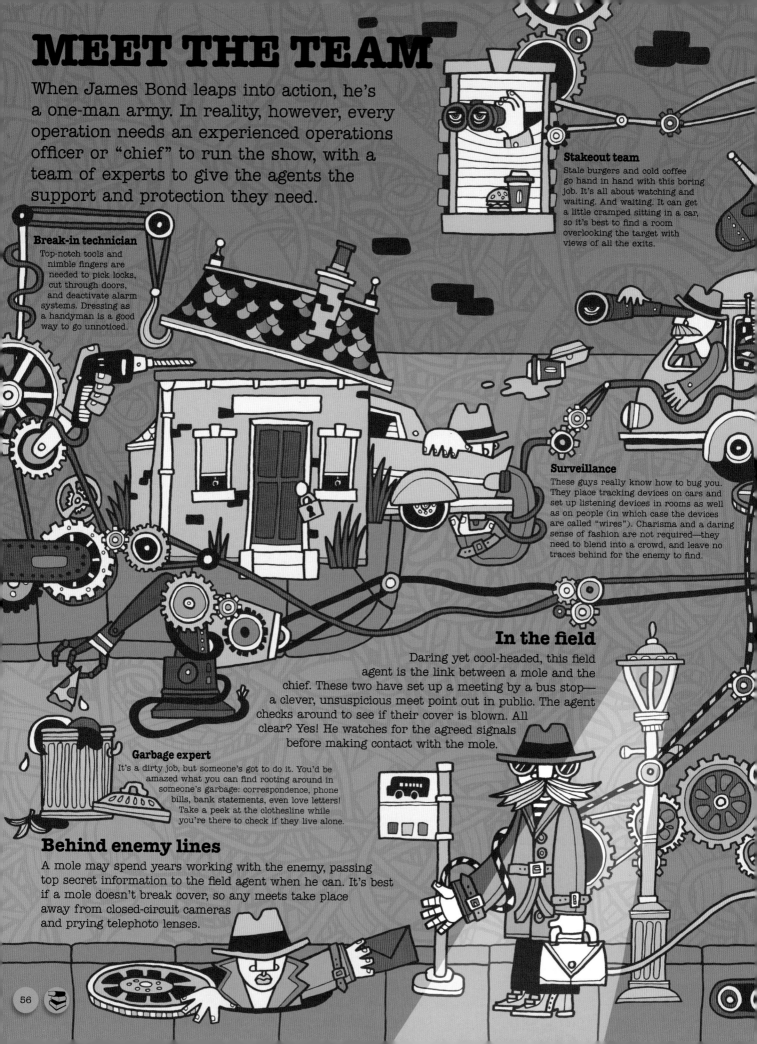

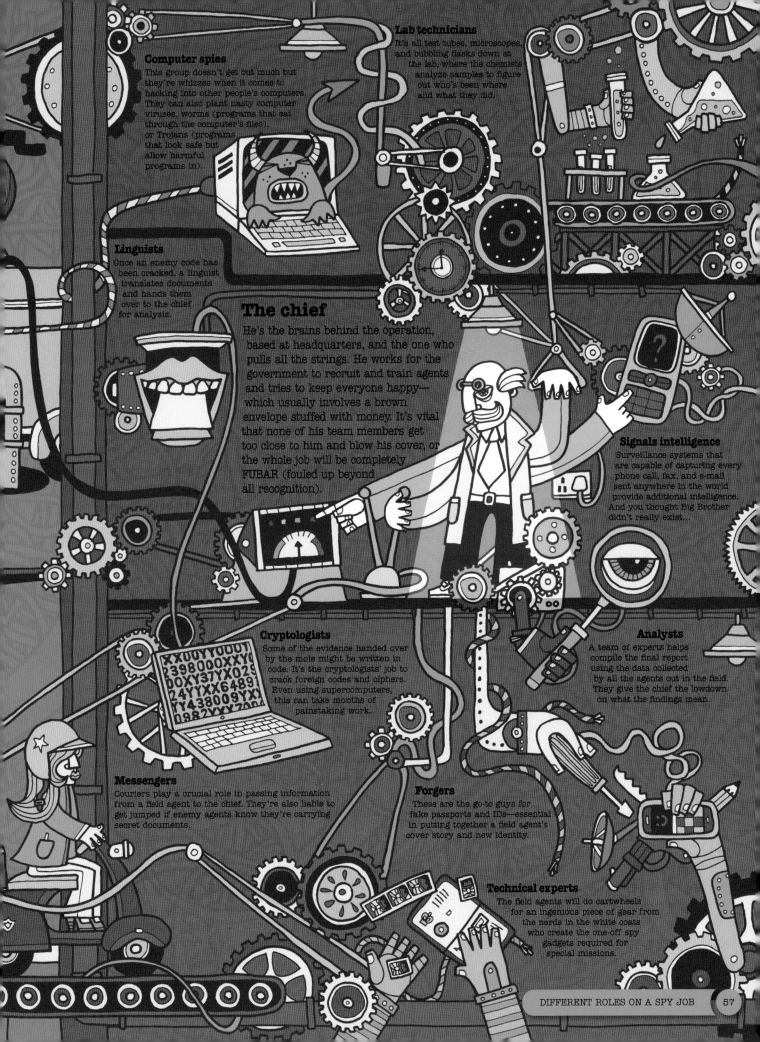

Computer spies

This group doesn't get out much but they're whizzes when it comes to hacking into other people's computers. They can also plant nasty computer viruses, worms (programs that eat through the computer's files), or Trojans (programs that look safe but allow harmful programs in).

Lab technicians

It's all test tubes, microscopes, and bubbling flasks down at the lab, where the chemists analyze samples to figure out who's been where and what they did.

Linguists

Once an enemy code has been cracked, a linguist translates documents and hands them over to the chief for analysis.

The chief

He's the brains behind the operation, based at headquarters, and the one who pulls all the strings. He works for the government to recruit and train agents and tries to keep everyone happy—which usually involves a brown envelope stuffed with money. It's vital that none of his team members get too close to him and blow his cover, or the whole job will be completely FUBAR (fouled up beyond all recognition).

Signals intelligence

Surveillance systems that are capable of capturing every phone call, fax, and e-mail sent anywhere in the world provide additional intelligence. And you thought Big Brother didn't really exist...

Cryptologists

Some of the evidence handed over by the mole might be written in code. It's the cryptologists' job to crack foreign codes and ciphers. Even using supercomputers, this can take months of painstaking work.

Analysts

A team of experts helps compile the final report using the data collected by all the agents out in the field. They give the chief the lowdown on what the findings mean.

Messengers

Couriers play a crucial role in passing information from a field agent to the chief. They're also liable to get jumped if enemy agents know they're carrying secret documents.

Forgers

These are the go-to guys for fake passports and IDs—essential in putting together a field agent's cover story and new identity.

Technical experts

The field agents will do cartwheels for an ingenious piece of gear from the nerds in the white coats who create the one-off spy gadgets required for special missions.

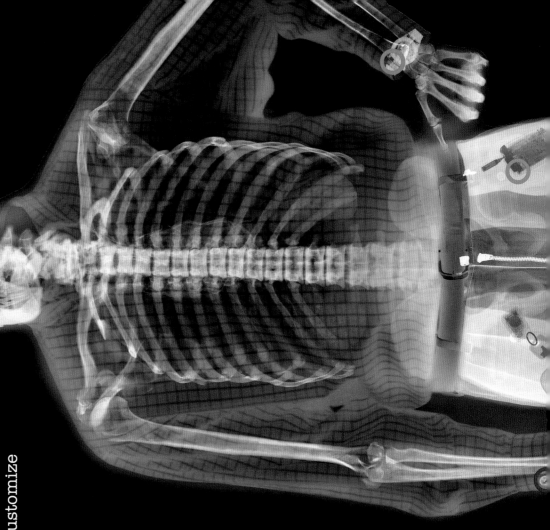

ART OF CONCEALMENT

Spies rely on a collection of increasingly sophisticated gadgets and gizmos to carry out their ops. They must be able to use them without attracting undue attention, and the gadgets should remain well hidden when not in use. One way to do this is to conceal them within everyday objects. A tube of lipstick, a phone battery, a coin, even a stick of chewing gum can double as a concealment device. Spy agencies employ teams of people to customize common objects and turn them into spy gear.

Sunglasses

On a shady mission? A pair of sunglasses can conceal a miniature video camera or a microphone to capture and amplify faraway conversations. A glasses case can also be utilized to hide items.

Watch this space

An ordinary wristwatch can contain a spy camera, tracking device, or video camera. The spy can pretend to check the time while secretly snapping a photograph. It also tells the time!

Pocket money

Coins can be hollowed out to hold a secret message. In a pocket full of change, a hollow coin would be nearly impossible to spot.

Phony phones

Cell phones can be equipped with all kinds of surveillance gadgets. Spies can activate cell-phone microphones remotely, so that they can listen in on nearby conversations. Does that bug you?

Buttons

Ordinary buttons can be replaced with mini-cameras. In World War II, British spies wore magnetized buttons. If lost, an agent could remove them and balance them on each other to make a compass.

Hidden pockets

Do you need a place to conceal classified data, hide that second passport, or stash your cash? Secret pockets in clothing and coat linings provide hard-to-spot hiding places. Likewise, false bottoms in suitcases and bags hide objects.

Pen and paper

Pens can contain recording devices as well as handy gadgets like lasers or lock picks. Books can be hollowed out to hold something, or the paper may be soaked in chemicals to smuggle the chemicals unnoticed.

Shoes and shoe heels

A secret compartment can be hollowed into the heel of a shoe. The insoles can also provide a secure, if smelly, hiding place for flat objects. In the Cold War, bugs were planted in shoe heels to record clandestine meetings. Something was afoot.

Hanky panky

During World War II, British spycraft expert Charles Fraser-Smith created a handkerchief that revealed a map when dropped in urine. It wasn't anything to sneeze at.

Card shark

The CIA invented a deck of playing cards that concealed a map. When the top layer of paper was soaked away from the cards, the map was revealed. Now that's a card trick!

Hair spray

A can of hair spray, the handle of a hairbrush, a tube of sunscreen, and many other toiletries and cosmetics can be decoy versions used as secret compartments. Hair-raising stuff!

Car and house keys

To unlock secrets as well as doors, car and house keys and key chains can be equipped with cameras and eavesdropping devices.

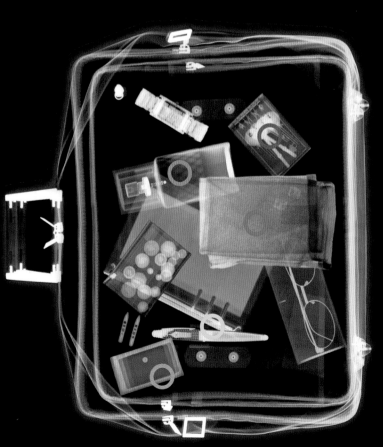

BRAIN GYM

A spy's most important weapon is the human brain. Spies need to take in lots of information quickly, and be able to retain and remember it. Some information is far too confidential to be written down, so having a good memory is essential. Scientists say that an average brain can hold about five to seven items in short-term memory at any one time. Spies train their brains using a number of simple techniques to help memorize larger amounts of information for longer. But there are some brainteasers to watch out for, too...

Visualization

This trick helps you remember numbers by associating them with shapes. For example, the number two resembles a swan, a zero looks like an egg, eight a snowman, and six a rabbit. So to remember 2086, imagine a swan laying an egg, which hatches into a snowman jumping up and down with a rabbit. Just try to forget that!

Nonsense sentences

You can make up a silly sentence in which the first letter of each word represents the initial of what you want to remember. For example, music students learn the phrase "every good boy does fine" to remind them of the notes in the treble clef: E, G, B, D, and F. These devices are called mnemonics.

Location

This trick will help you remember a long list of seemingly unrelated steps, such as what you need to prepare for a birthday party. First, think of a familiar location or journey, such as your room or trip to school. Next, mentally "place" the items in sequence around that location or along the route.

Photographic memory

Eidetic memory—the ability to recall a vast amount of information with accuracy—is so rare that some experts think it doesn't actually exist, and that people who claim to have it are just using complex mnemonic techniques. The ability to take a "mental photograph" of a scene and remember it in detail is certainly an asset in spying—that's a no-brainer.

Chunking

Breaking information down into smaller parts to help you remember it is called chunking. For example, it's very difficult to memorize a long string of numbers, but if you first group the numbers into sets of three, it will be much easier. Chunking turns the limits of short-term memory to your advantage—a weight off your mind.

Mix it up

By making changes to your daily routine or by learning new things, you will use brain pathways that you weren't using before. Simply brushing your teeth with your nondominant hand can light up connections in your brain. Learning a new language or instrument is another way to exercise your gray matter.

Brain wiping

Sometimes, remembering everything isn't such a good thing. Beta blockers are drugs that are used to treat high blood pressure. Scientists have found that they may also help people who have had distressing experiences to block their bad memories. A substance in the drug halts the neurotransmitters in the brain that lay down memories. There are concerns, however, that brain-wiping drugs could be misued on people who have no reason to want to forget.

Brainwashing

This is the name for a method of extreme persuasion, where people use manipulative methods to persuade others to change their beliefs. While typical brainwashing techniques can certainly affect a person's mental health and behavior, many scientists think that there is no evidence to support the idea of mind control.

False memories

In the 1990s, a sudden wave of "recovered memory" cases (for example, people "remembering" that they had been victims of abuse) hit the United States. Psychologists who investigated the phenomenon showed that memory can be manipulated through hypnosis or sedatives, making people "remember" things that never happened.

AVOIDING SURVEILLANCE

Do you ever feel the hairs on the back of your neck stand on end when you think someone's watching you? There are hairy times aplenty for a spy under surveillance, whether they know they're being watched (as in overt surveillance) or not (covert surveillance). But spies are trained to identify spy-spotters and can usually give them the slip...

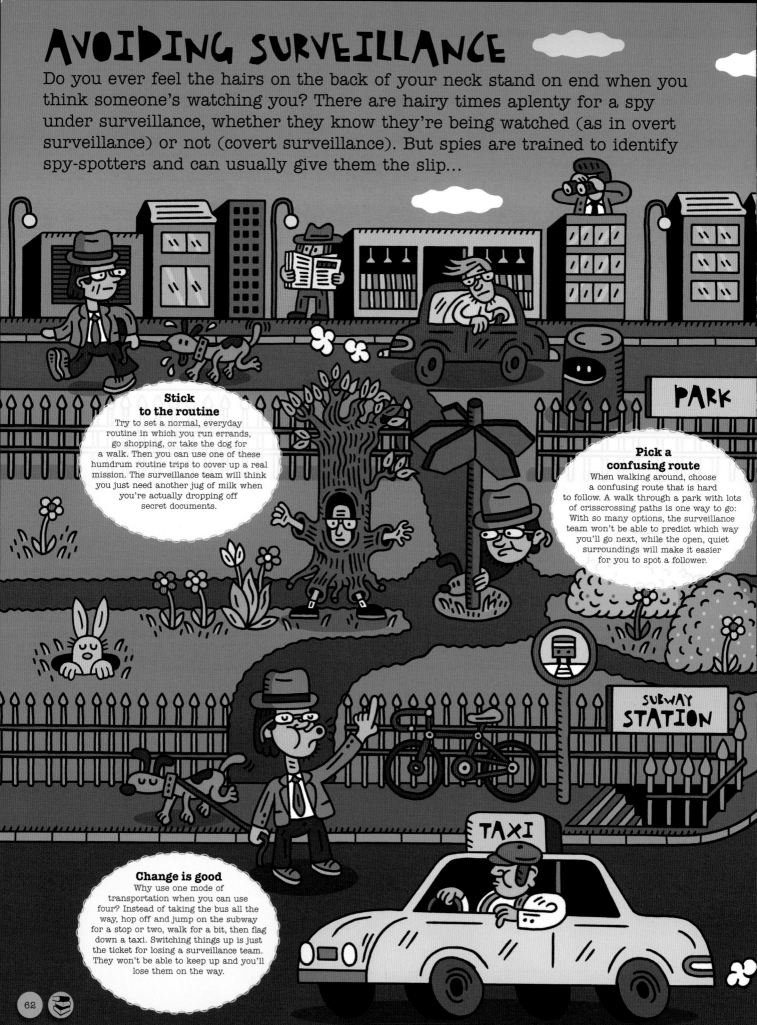

Stick to the routine
Try to set a normal, everyday routine in which you run errands, go shopping, or take the dog for a walk. Then you can use one of these humdrum routine trips to cover up a real mission. The surveillance team will think you just need another jug of milk when you're actually dropping off secret documents.

Pick a confusing route
When walking around, choose a confusing route that is hard to follow. A walk through a park with lots of crisscrossing paths is one way to go: With so many options, the surveillance team won't be able to predict which way you'll go next, while the open, quiet surroundings will make it easier for you to spot a follower.

Change is good
Why use one mode of transportation when you can use four? Instead of taking the bus all the way, hop off and jump on the subway for a stop or two, walk for a bit, then flag down a taxi. Switching things up is just the ticket for losing a surveillance team. They won't be able to keep up and you'll lose them on the way.

PARK

SUBWAY STATION

TAXI

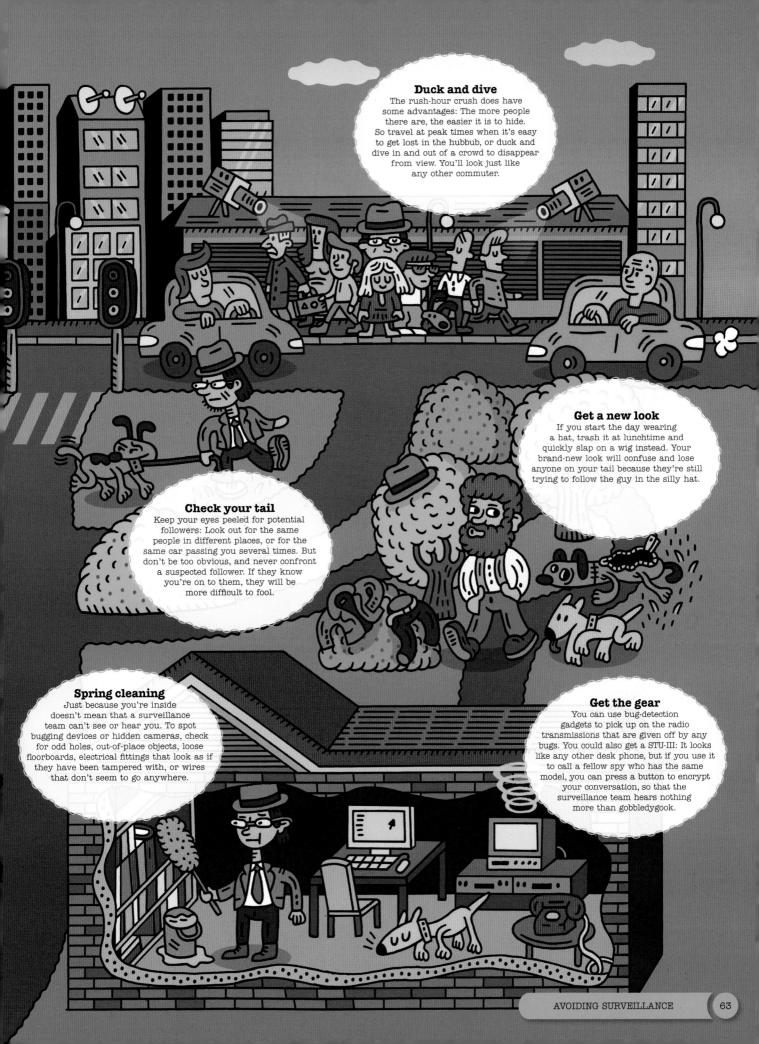

Duck and dive
The rush-hour crush does have some advantages: The more people there are, the easier it is to hide. So travel at peak times when it's easy to get lost in the hubbub, or duck and dive in and out of a crowd to disappear from view. You'll look just like any other commuter.

Get a new look
If you start the day wearing a hat, trash it at lunchtime and quickly slap on a wig instead. Your brand-new look will confuse and lose anyone on your tail because they're still trying to follow the guy in the silly hat.

Check your tail
Keep your eyes peeled for potential followers: Look out for the same people in different places, or for the same car passing you several times. But don't be too obvious, and never confront a suspected follower. If they know you're on to them, they will be more difficult to fool.

Spring cleaning
Just because you're inside doesn't mean that a surveillance team can't see or hear you. To spot bugging devices or hidden cameras, check for odd holes, out-of-place objects, loose floorboards, electrical fittings that look as if they have been tampered with, or wires that don't seem to go anywhere.

Get the gear
You can use bug-detection gadgets to pick up on the radio transmissions that are given off by any bugs. You could also get a STU-III: It looks like any other desk phone, but if you use it to call a fellow spy who has the same model, you can press a button to encrypt your conversation, so that the surveillance team hears nothing more than gobbledygook.

DROP-DEAD DEVIOUS

When it's too dangerous or difficult to meet in person, spies can pass messages or objects to one another via a prearranged hiding place called a dead drop. These are often found in public locations, and items for exchange are placed in various devices to protect and conceal them. The best dead-drop devices blend in without attracting much notice. Once you know what to look for, it's a walk in the park.

Submerged secrets

Have you got something fishy to hide? The murky depths of lakes and rivers provide good hiding places, but the data must be protected from water damage. Walletlike waterproof pouches with metal weights help your secret package stay nice and dry and sink to the bottom so that it doesn't float away.

Secure spikes

Hollow metal spikes, resembling big pencils with screw caps, are good dead-drop devices. The package is stashed inside the cavity and then the spike is pushed into the earth in any soft, grassy area. The East German intelligence agency, the HVA, often hid such spikes in graveyards—because people visit graveyards at irregular times, the agents just looked like any other visitors.

Loaded logs

In the 1950s, the Australian intelligence agency, ASIS, communicated with a KGB double agent via a wooden-log dead drop. It looked like any other piece of firewood, but when the agent removed a nail in the log, a spring-loaded plug popped out to reveal a sealed tube for messages.

Digital drops

Virtual dead drops are just as effective as real ones. An agent might use a wireless router as a dead drop, encoding messages that can be picked up by nearby users who know how to access them. A message can also be left on an encrypted website or in an e-mail drafts folder. Then another agent who knows the password can pick up the message wherever they are in the world.

Subtle signpost

Spies leave a signal to let the other party know that there is something to be retrieved. They might mark a tree with chalk, move a potted plant on a balcony... whatever doesn't draw attention. Typically, a signal should not be near the dead-drop site—it could be an ad in the paper. An all-clear signal confirms that the material has been collected.

Stuffed animals

The CIA has used dead rats to stash secret messages. The rats were hollowed out, stuffed with secrets, and left for pickup. To keep other animals from nibbling them, the rodents were painted with hot chili sauce. No one smelled a rat.

Rock-solid idea

The Soviet GRU used fake rocks to drop messages to its undercover agents who were stationed in the United States in the late 1970s. The rocks were specially designed to look like the real rocks in the area—a rock-solid idea.

SEEING STARS

Dahling! Cast your eyes over this all-star cast of celebrities. Legends in their own fields, these A-listers also did fieldwork for leading spy agencies. Some volunteered, but others were recruited for various reasons: their access to the powerful, their knowledge of the world, the cover their fame offered—and their all-around fabulousness.

MOE BERG

This American baseball player wasn't the best on his team, but he may have been the brightest, speaking six languages. In 1934, he joined a team touring Japan but he didn't play ball; in Tokyo, he took secret pictures of the harbor and weapons factories, which were used to plan U.S. bombing raids in 1942.

HEDY LAMARR

This Viennese-born silver-screen sensation later moved to Hollywood. During World War II, she and a friend patented a secret communication system, known as frequency hopping, to help make radio-guided torpedoes harder to locate. This idea was later used in military communications, wireless phones, and Wi-Fi.

CARY GRANT

The ultimate leading man, Cary Grant was born Archibald Leach in England. In Hollywood, he monitored suspected Nazi sympathizers and reported information back to British spymasters.

JOSEPHINE BAKER

Born in the United States, Baker became a popular entertainer in Paris. She helped the French Resistance during World War II by smuggling secrets written in invisible ink on her sheet music. Starstruck customs officials never suspected a thing, and her entourage (including other members of the French Resistance) crossed borders without trouble.

IAN FLEMING

The creator of James Bond learned about spying firsthand in British Naval Intelligence during World War II. He was the commander behind several espionage missions, including "Operation Goldeneye"—a plan to keep British communications open with Gibraltar, if Spain entered the war.

JULIA CHILD

Before becoming one of America's most famous chefs, Child worked for the Office of Strategic Services (OSS). Posted to Washington, Sri Lanka, and China, she was in charge of keeping track of the most secret operatives. She also cooked up a shark repellent to prevent sharks from bumping into underwater explosives.

JOHN FORD

American movie director John Ford also made documentaries for the OSS, filming combat operations and military installations. The movies (some of which were so secret they were shown only once) were screened to provide intelligence, as well as to train troops and boost morale.

ANNA CHAPMAN

The odd one out, Anna Chapman actually became famous for spying after she and nine other Russian sleeper agents were deported from the United States, in 2010, in exchange for a ring of U.S. agents working in Russia. Chapman soon became a celebrity in Moscow, hosting a television talk show, posing for a Russian magazine cover, and having a sing-along with Vladimir Putin.

WALT DISNEY

In 1955, American entertainment icon Walt Disney became an official FBI contact, reporting information to the Los Angeles branch. He may have been asked to supply the agency with the names of Communist sympathizers in Hollywood, ratting out his colleagues in the movie industry.

CHARMED, I'M SURE

One of the most useful traits a spy can possess is a charming personality. You can't judge a book by its cover, of course, but an attractive, charismatic person may influence and persuade others more easily. Would-be spies should take a leaf out of these spies' books. They whispered sweet nothings in exchange for state secrets... resistance was futile.

HITLER'S SOCIALITE

Dashing Dmitri

Dmitri Bystrolytov

This dashing, aristocratic Soviet spy spoke almost 20 languages, but the one he was most fluent in was the language of love. Bystrolytov (1901–1975) enthralled an array of women during World War II, including a German countess, a French diplomat, and the wife of a British official. Despite providing a steady supply of European secrets, he was imprisoned by the suspicious Soviet authorities.

Princess Stephanie Julianna von Hohenlohe

Austrian-born Stephanie (1891–1972) married into German royalty. She lived in London between the two world wars, mingling with the cream of British society. The secrets she charmed out of cabinet members and other officials ended up in the hands of her great friend, Adolf Hitler. During World War II, she fled to the United States where an official memo described her as a threat that was "worse than 10,000 men."

CALL ME CYNTHIA

Amy Elizabeth Thorpe

Something of a man magnet, American Thorpe (1910–1963) enchanted diplomats in Washington, D.C., before marrying a British official who she conducted secret operations with during the Spanish Civil War. Working for British intelligence, Thorpe returned to Washington, where she stole secret codebooks from the Vichy embassy (the government of Nazi-occupied France) while undercover as a journalist named Cynthia.

TOP SECRET

Pei Pu

...e inspiration behind Madame ...tterfly, Shi (1938–2009) was not ...she, but a male opera singer who taught Chinese to French diplomats. Shi convinced French embassy worker Monsieur Boursicot that he was a woman forced to live as a man, and the pair had a 20-year affair while Shi obtained state secrets.

Roald Dahl

During World War II, British fighter pilot Dahl (1916–1990) was sent to the United States, where powerful men and influential women shared their secrets with him as he snooped for British intelligence. While still working in the spy business, he also became a children's author.

Fantastic Mr. Foxy

Madame Butterfly

Birds of a feather

During the Cold War, the Soviet Union's KGB trained female spies to entice U.S. agents and officers. The women, known as swallows, seduced their targets and extracted information from the smitten men by blackmailing them. Their male equivalents were known as ravens.

Hello, Romeo

Romeos

During the Cold War, the East German secret police recruited a team of handsome, intelligent male spies, nicknamed "Romeos," to seek out female secretaries with access to the West's secrets. They piled on the charm and successfully extracted key pieces of information.

Charlotte de Beaune Semblançay

Charlotte (1551–1617) was one of French queen-mother Catherine de Medici's beautiful female spies, who collected information from adoring men in her court. On Catherine's instructions, Charlotte became mistress and confidante to Catherine's son-in-law, French king Henry of Navarre.

LA REINE MARGOT

A swallow's tale

WHO ARE YOU?

It's a simple question, but one that a spy may not want to answer. Assuming an alias and posing as a completely different person is a useful tool for spy work. Pretending to be someone else gives spies a story to keep their true intentions under wraps. Here are some of the ways a spy may create a new identity.

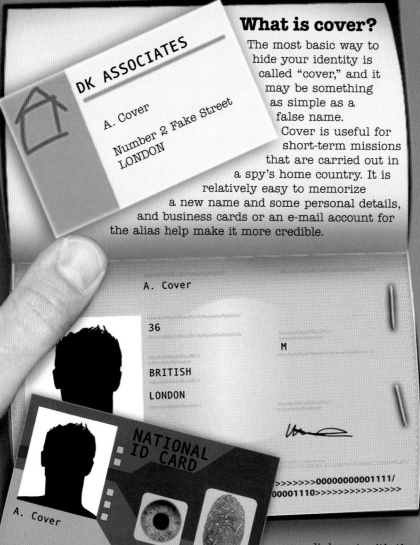

What is cover?

The most basic way to hide your identity is called "cover," and it may be something as simple as a false name.

Cover is useful for short-term missions that are carried out in a spy's home country. It is relatively easy to memorize a new name and some personal details, and business cards or an e-mail account for the alias help make it more credible.

What is a legend?

For more complex or long-term missions, cover does not provide enough protection and an entire fake biography, called a legend, must be invented to support the cover. The spy's invented life history is imagined and painstakingly put together in great detail. Establishing a legend takes time, though. The more high-risk the mission, the better the legend must be.

Who needs it?

Not all spies operate under the protection of a cover or legend. For example, the CIA employs around 20,000 people, of which less than 10 percent are directly involved in secret ops, where a cover might be useful. Those who do participate in secret ops, however, may have more than one secret identity to fall back on.

Officially covered

A spy working abroad is most commonly given "official cover"—a phony job as a diplomat with the government's embassy or at another official office. No one would be too suspicious of a diplomat meeting with top officials or asking difficult questions. "Non-official covers," or NOCs, on the other hand, are for those spies on the most secret missions, where even their presence needs to be covered up, or for those whose lives could be at stake if their true identities emerged.

Creating the legend

Passports, paperwork, and photographs must all be faked to support the legend. Skilled teams working at spy agencies can duplicate even the most copy-proof papers. Spies carry "pocket litter"— ticket stubs, coins, and receipts—to bolster their imaginary image. It takes time and skill to create the perfect legend, and in many cases, the spy may live the double life for years before being "activated" on the mission.

Living the lie

The spy will need to remember every detail of the legend and play the role convincingly. In today's web-based social-networking frenzy, the spy needs a convincing visual past to post online, too.

With the constant risk of tripping up over details, the spy living the legend must always be "on"—unlike an actor, they cannot break cover, even for a second. Living a legend is tough and stressful work, and in some cases, a bout of forgetfulness can have fatal consequences.

RETURN
VIA: PARIS
DATE: 25/0

SPY WEAR

If you snooped in a spy's wardrobe, what would you find? The clothing and accessories that spies wear can help them conceal their identities so that they can operate without drawing undue attention. Clothing can also support a cover story, such as in wartime when a spy might slip into an enemy uniform. There's no disguising it: The right wardrobe is a key part of spying.

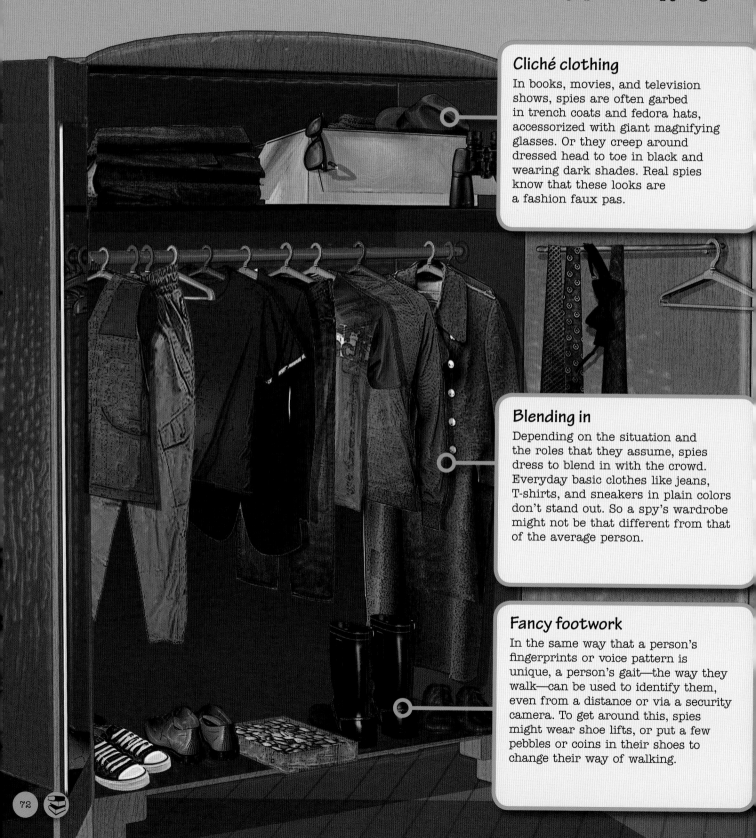

Cliché clothing

In books, movies, and television shows, spies are often garbed in trench coats and fedora hats, accessorized with giant magnifying glasses. Or they creep around dressed head to toe in black and wearing dark shades. Real spies know that these looks are a fashion faux pas.

Blending in

Depending on the situation and the roles that they assume, spies dress to blend in with the crowd. Everyday basic clothes like jeans, T-shirts, and sneakers in plain colors don't stand out. So a spy's wardrobe might not be that different from that of the average person.

Fancy footwork

In the same way that a person's fingerprints or voice pattern is unique, a person's gait—the way they walk—can be used to identify them, even from a distance or via a security camera. To get around this, spies might wear shoe lifts, or put a few pebbles or coins in their shoes to change their way of walking.

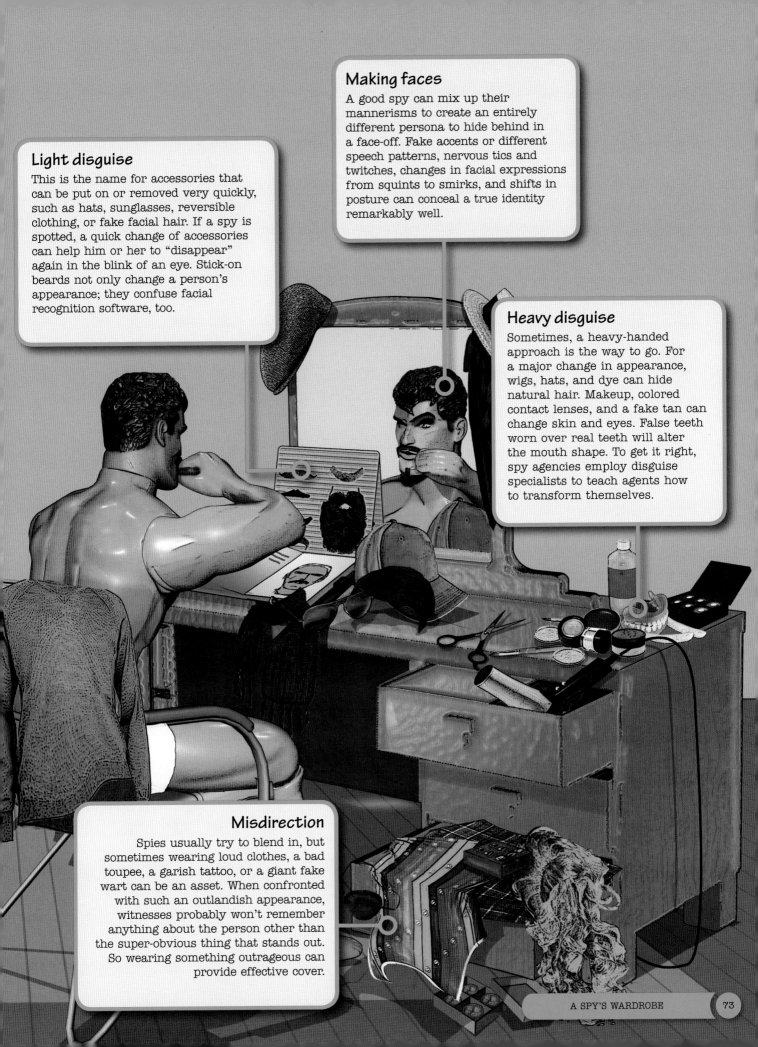

Light disguise

This is the name for accessories that can be put on or removed very quickly, such as hats, sunglasses, reversible clothing, or fake facial hair. If a spy is spotted, a quick change of accessories can help him or her to "disappear" again in the blink of an eye. Stick-on beards not only change a person's appearance; they confuse facial recognition software, too.

Making faces

A good spy can mix up their mannerisms to create an entirely different persona to hide behind in a face-off. Fake accents or different speech patterns, nervous tics and twitches, changes in facial expressions from squints to smirks, and shifts in posture can conceal a true identity remarkably well.

Heavy disguise

Sometimes, a heavy-handed approach is the way to go. For a major change in appearance, wigs, hats, and dye can hide natural hair. Makeup, colored contact lenses, and a fake tan can change skin and eyes. False teeth worn over real teeth will alter the mouth shape. To get it right, spy agencies employ disguise specialists to teach agents how to transform themselves.

Misdirection

Spies usually try to blend in, but sometimes wearing loud clothes, a bad toupee, a garish tattoo, or a giant fake wart can be an asset. When confronted with such an outlandish appearance, witnesses probably won't remember anything about the person other than the super-obvious thing that stands out. So wearing something outrageous can provide effective cover.

LONDON, 1810. PEOPLE GATHER AROUND A BED IN A DINGY FLAT. THE LOCAL DOCTOR ANNOUNCES THE NEWS.

IT'S A BOY!

IT'S NOT A BIRTH, BUT A BOMBSHELL: FOR NEARLY HALF A CENTURY, THE MYSTERY MAN WHO DIED IN THIS ROOM HAD LIVED... AS A WOMAN! SHE WAS CHEVALIER D'EON, MASTER/MISTRESS OF DECEPTION, SECRET AGENT, AND THE TALK OF THE TOWN.

WELL I'LL BE DARNED, D'EON WAS A MAN.

THERE GOES MY BET.

GASP!

BORN CHARLES-GENEVIÈVE-LOUIS-AUGUSTE-ANDRÉ-TIMOTHÉE D'EON DE BEAUMONT IN 1728, THE YOUNG D'EON WAS AMONG THE BEST STUDENTS IN BURGUNDY, IF NOT ALL OF FRANCE. HIS REMARKABLE MEMORY AND GIFT FOR LANGUAGES EARNED HIM A PLACE AT LAW SCHOOL.

TO PARIS WITH YOU, MY BEST PUPIL, WITH A FUTURE AS BRIGHT AS ITS GLITTERING CITY LIGHTS. I ENVY YOU.

THANK YOU, SIR. BUT I WILL NOT FORGET WHO I AM.

D'EON GRADUATED FROM LAW SCHOOL, THEN WORKED AS A ROYAL OFFICIAL. IN 1756, HE WAS TAPPED TO JOIN THE SECRET DU ROI–KING LOUIS XV'S NETWORK OF SPIES WHO REPORTED DIRECTLY TO THE THRONE.

YOU UNDERSTAND WE WORK OUTSIDE THE GOVERNMENT AND ITS RULES. IN "THE SECRET," WE KEEP SECRETS.

I WILL HONOR THE KING'S WISHES.

WELCOME TO THE CLUB!

IT WAS ALL THE RAGE FOR UPPER-CLASS WOMEN AND MEN TO SWITCH ROLES AT FANCY PARTIES. NOTICING THAT D'EON CUT A PARTICULARLY FINE FIGURE IN A DRESS, LOUIS SENT D'EON TO MOSCOW, WHERE EMPRESS ELIZABETH I WAS FAMED FOR HER ROLE-SWITCHING PARTIES, TO HELP THAW THE ICY RELATIONS BETWEEN FRANCE AND RUSSIA.

WITHIN THE RUSSIAN IMPERIAL COURT, D'EON APPEARED AT ONE OF ELIZABETH'S MASKED BALLS AS A LADY. SOON "SHE" WAS A FAVORITE AT COURT.

IT IS AN HONOR TO BE HERE, EMPRESS ELIZABETH.

YOU, MON AMIE, ARE THE BELLE OF THE BALL. PLEASE CONVEY OUR BEST WISHES TO YOUR KING. CHARMING DRESS!

THIS IS WORKING LIKE A CHARM.

D'EON RETURNED HOME TO FRANCE IN 1761, WITH DIPLOMATIC RELATIONS BETWEEN THE NATIONS RESTORED. OVER THE NEXT YEAR, WHILE D'EON FOUGHT IN THE DRAGOONS (HORSE-MOUNTED TROOPS) DURING THE SEVEN-YEAR WAR THAT RAVAGED EUROPE, "THE SECRET" HATCHED A NEW PLAN FOR D'EON...

LOUIS IS PONDERING WHETHER OR NOT TO INVADE ENGLAND... I SAY WE SEND D'EON TO ASSESS THE SITUATION.

HE CAN POSE AS A TEMPORARY AMBASSADOR.

HIS DRAGOON UNIFORM WILL MARK HIM AS A MAN OF HONOR...

HE'S QUITE FOND OF DRESSING UP, ISN'T HE?

D'EON'S SHIP ARRIVED IN LONDON IN 1763 AND HE EMBRACED HIS NEW ROLE, UNDERCOVER AS THE FRENCH AMBASSADOR'S SECRETARY, WHILE SPYING FOR LOUIS BACK HOME, AND WAS SOON MOVING IN THE MOST ELITE CIRCLES.

BY LAVISHING EXPENSIVE GIFTS OF BURGUNDY WINE ON IMPORTANT AND INFLUENTIAL BRITS, D'EON WON OVER SEVERAL MEMBERS OF THE RULING CLASS.

WHAT FINE FRENCH WINE! MARVELOUS PRESENT, DEAR CHAP. I WON'T FORGET YOUR KIND GENEROSITY...

IF HE SAMPLES ANY MORE, HE WON'T REMEMBER A THING!

WITH D'EON'S DEBTS MOUNTING AS HE WORKED ENGLAND'S UPPER CIRCLES, THE ONLY THING HIGHER THAN HIS WINE BILL WAS HIS EXPECTATION OF BECOMING THE REAL FRENCH AMBASSADOR. BUT HIS RIVAL, COMTE DE GUERCHY, GOT THE JOB, AND THE FRENCH DEMANDED D'EON'S RETURN. NOT ONLY DID HE REFUSE—HE PLANNED TO BETRAY KING LOUIS...

D'EON THREATENED TO TELL ALL ABOUT LOUIS'S SECRET INVASION PLANS, ABOUT WHICH THE FRENCH GOVERNMENT KNEW NOTHING. ALSO, IN AN ATTEMPT TO DISGRACE GUERCHY, HE SAID THAT THE AMBASSADOR HAD TRIED TO POISON HIM! BUT AFTER CIRCULATING SUCH GOSSIP HE NEEDED A COVER... HE STARTED A RUMOR THAT HE WAS REALLY A WOMAN. SURELY THE KING'S SPIES WOULDN'T HARM A WOMAN...

WHEN IN DISTRESS, PUT ON A DRESS.

WAS HE A SHE? THE QUESTION ABOUT D'EON'S REAL GENDER WAS THE HOTTEST GOSSIP IN LONDON. ITS COFFEEHOUSES BUZZED WITH RUMOR AND SPECULATION. THE LONDON STOCK EXCHANGE EVEN TOOK BETS ON THE SUBJECT!

HAVE YOU SEEN HER HANDS? I WAGER THOSE ARE A MAN'S MITTS.

GET IN QUICK—THE ODDS ARE ABOUT TO CHANGE.

I SAY SHE'S A LADY. MAYBE ODD, BUT DEFINITELY FEMALE.

IN THE CLAMOR OF SPECULATION OVER D'EON'S CLAIMS, THE KING, FACING HUMILIATION OVER HIS UNVEILED SPYING AND INVASION PLANS, FINALLY AGREED TO PAY D'EON'S DEBTS. BUT ONLY ON THE CONDITION THAT D'EON WOULDN'T PUBLISH THE KING'S LETTERS, WHICH CONFIRMED THE CLAIMS, AND THAT D'EON RETURN TO FRANCE... IN WOMEN'S CLOTHING.

THIS IS A PROBLEM I CAN NO LONGER SKIRT.

BACK IN BURGUNDY, D'EON WAS UNHAPPY AND UNSETTLED— ONCE A RESPECTED DRAGOON VETERAN, HE PROTESTED AGAINST HIS FEMALE LOT BY SPORTING A FIVE-O'-CLOCK SHADOW, WHILE HIS GARB OF BLACK DRESSES REFLECTED HIS OUT-OF-PLACE FEELINGS. HE WAS FINALLY ALLOWED TO RETURN TO LONDON, BUT WAS STILL REQUIRED TO DRESS IN WOMEN'S CLOTHES.

D'EON CAUSED A SENSATION. IN PUBLIC, HE KEPT ON DOING ALL-MALE THINGS, BUT IN A DRESS! HE RACED UP STAIRS, FENCED WITH PEOPLE FOR MONEY, AND SERVED WOMEN IN COFFEEHOUSES (A JOB FOR MEN AT THE TIME). AS SUCH, HE WAS A ONE-MAN LONDON TOURIST ATTRACTION.

I'LL GIVE YOU A DRESSING DOWN!

YOU MAY BE A BLADE, BUT YOUR WIT IS LESS THAN RAZOR SHARP.

IN PRIVATE, D'EON COLLECTED A LIBRARY OF BOOKS EXPLORING THE ROLE OF FEMALES IN SOCIETY. HIS EXPERIENCE OF LIVING AS A MAN AND A WOMAN HAD TURNED HIM INTO AN EARLY FEMINIST, UNHAPPY WITH THE DICTATED ROLES AND LIMITATIONS IMPOSED UPON FEMALES.

AFTER 49 YEARS AS A MAN AND 34 AS A WOMAN, D'EON'S EXTRAORDINARY LIFE CAME TO AN END. A DOCTOR CONDUCTING THE POSTMORTEM FINALLY ENDED THE 40-YEAR SPECULATION ON D'EON'S GENDER...

LET'S LAY THE MATTER TO REST, AND MAY SHE REST IN PEACE... OR RATHER, HE!

WHEN HE PULLED A DRESS OVER HIS HEAD, D'EON PULLED THE WOOL OVER PEOPLE'S EYES AND FOOLED PEOPLE THE WORLD OVER. HIS WAS THE ULTIMATE COVER STORY.

SURVIVING CAPTURE

Only bad spies get caught—so the saying goes. But espionage is a risky business, with many factors out of a spy's control, such as being betrayed by a mole or a defector from a foreign intelligence service. Spies are constantly living on the edge, within a whisker of exposure. If they are captured, they must be "neutralized" so that they can no longer spy. This can mean something as simple as a trip home… or something much nastier.

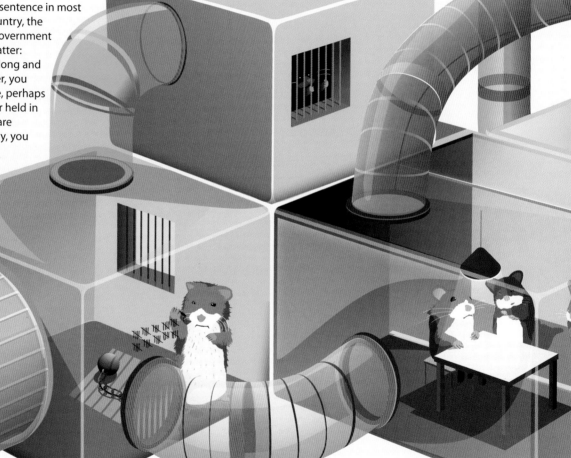

What happens next?

You will be behind bars quicker than you can say "hamster!" But for how long? That depends. If you are caught spying on your own country, you may be tried for treason, which involves a lengthy sentence in most countries. In a foreign country, the relations between your government and your host country matter: If the two countries get along and you have diplomatic cover, you may simply be sent home, perhaps in exchange for a prisoner held in your own country. If you are caught in a hostile country, you can expect a harsher fate.

Preparing for the worst

Spies are made aware of what might happen if they are captured, and told how to behave when facing the worst kinds of punishment. Life-threatening situations are, after all, part of the job description. Spies are briefed on a range of survival strategies to give them the mental tools to survive. If facing a long stretch behind bars, for example, exercise helps release the body's natural antidepressant, adrenaline.

Questions, questions

Following capture, a spy is most likely to face interrogation— a very skilled type of questioning to get information, in which the interrogator is always in control and leads the "conversation." Interrogators use several techniques, from the threat of physical harm and making the captive as uncomfortable as possible to putting him at ease so that he lets his guard down. Eventually, the captive may squeak.

Would I lie to you?

"Lie detector" machines called polygraphs measure physical changes in the human body, such as heart rate, blood pressure, and sweatiness. A captured spy might be wired up while being interrogated so that their physical response to each question can be monitored.

Tortured times

Information can be extracted by inflicting pain on someone to break their will. There are all kinds of horrendous devices for causing physical pain, while psychological techniques like sleep deprivation, relentless loud noise, isolation, and ultra-bright lights can create mental confusion.

It's a killer

Some spies choose to kill themselves rather than risk compromising their mission. During World War II, some spies carried pills, or devices like poison-tipped pins, so that they could commit suicide rather than face interrogation. Soviet-official-turned-CIA-spy Alexander Ogorodnik, for example, asked for his personal pen to write his confession when captured by the KGB. He swiftly extracted a cyanide pill from the top, swallowed it, and died instantly without revealing a single thing.

Double trouble

Sometimes, captured spies may be offered another option by their hosts: They will be released from captivity if they agree to become double agents. The threat of torture or execution is the most common way to make a spy see double. A redoubled agent is one who gets caught as a double agent and is forced to mislead foreign intelligence.

Escape!

A bold, brave, and physically resilient spy may take the risky move of escaping from captivity. Escaping takes daring, determination, and a roll-with-it attitude to adapt to every circumstance. Once out of sight, the spy must lie low and evade recapture, since the outlook for a recaptured spy is a grim one.

CRACKING CODES

Codes and ciphers make the spy world go round. They are the key to keeping secrets safe, and cracking them to reveal the hidden messages of a rival spy group is a pivotal part of the spy game. From word-mixing machines to digital dead drops, there are all kinds of devices to keep the code makers and breakers on their toes.

CRYPTIC CODES

Pssssst... boys and girls, can you keep a secret? Maybe. What if you need to pass that secret to another person? How do you keep the secret a secret in transit? There are various ways to hide and protect information. The science of keeping secrets secure is called cryptography, and the people who change letters and words into a code or cipher are known as cryptographers.

Playground rules

When using CODES, you must replace whole words or phrases with a letter, number, or symbol. Codes are decoded with a codebook.

When using CIPHERS, you must replace each letter with another letter. Ciphers are deciphered with a key.

CAESAR SHIFT

Roman general Julius Caesar wanted to get messages to his troops on the battlefield without the enemy finding out. He invented one of the first ciphers. Each letter in the message was replaced with another letter three places down in the alphabet.

ONE OF AL KINDI

This ninth-century Arab scholar wrote a book on codes and was the first person to describe frequency analysis. This is a method for figuring out how often letters appear to help break ciphers. With Al Kindi's advice, code breaking was like child's play.

ITALIAN JOB

Leon Battista Alberti (1404–1472) was an all-around clever Italian. In addition to being a musician and architect, he invented a rotating alphabetical disk to create a complex cipher, as well as a form of cipher that used two alphabets at the same time. Bravo!

WHAT A SQUARE!

French diplomat Blaise de Vigenère (1523–1596) learned about codes and ciphers during trips to Rome. He created a complex cipher with the letters arranged in a square, similar to a word search puzzle. To the untrained eye, the cipher appeared unsolvable. Goal!

ROYAL MYSTERY

The Great Cipher of French king Louis XIV remained a secret for almost 150 years. It was eventually broken by army code breaker Etienne Bazeries (1846–1931). He figured out that each number stood for a syllable, rather than a letter. Bazeries certainly kept his eye on the ball.

WIND TALKERS

During World War II, the language of the Native American Navajo tribe was used to create a code. Trained in pairs, young volunteers exchanged radio messages based on their little-known language. Their work helped defeat the Japanese, who never did crack the code.

MORSE OF COURSE

Samuel Morse (1791–1872) was an American who created a telegraph machine that sent electrical currents down a wire. He developed a code where each letter was represented by dots (short pulses) and dashes (longer ones). Most famously, his code was used to send a distress call from the Titanic.

TITANIC

SECRET-MESSAGE MACHINES

For as long as there has been war and politics, there has been a need for secret messages—to keep troops informed or to protect state secrets. Each of the machines featured here can be used for encoding and decoding words, and will take the original message, known as plaintext, and turn it into a jumbled-up message for safe sending.

POPULAR MODELS

There are two basic types of ciphers. A substitution cipher changes the letters in a message to another set of letters, or "cipher alphabet." The other type of cipher is known as a transposition cipher, which shuffles the letters around in a seemingly random way.

Variations on a theme

In the simplest form of substitution cipher, only one cipher alphabet is used throughout the message. In the cipher shown here, there is a shift that moves each character four places ahead in the alphabet. A polyalphabetic cipher, however, uses two or more alphabets at the same time.

A B C D E F G H I J K L M N O...

A B C D E F G H I J K L M N O P Q R...

WOODEN CIPHER

Thomas Jefferson's very own cipher wheel was developed in 1795 and features a stack of 26 turning wheels mounted on an axle. Each wheel has the alphabet written along its edge in random order. The machine is ideal for encrypting short messages.

CM 0001 All-wood Cipher Machine No batteries required

WITH FOLD-OUT SQUARE OF POSSIBLE COMBOS!

MORSE CODE TAPPER

In Morse code, letters and numbers are represented by short and long electrical signals. Tapping a machine like this transmits these "dots and dashes" and the message is received on a grooved strip of paper printed from a receiver. Skilled operators will be able to translate signals in their heads.

MC 0023 Code Tapper
Buy two for the price of one

MAKE A DASH FOR THIS SPECIAL OFFER

KRYHA

Invented by Ukrainian Alexander von Kryha in 1924, this machine uses a pair of alphabet wheels to encrypt plaintext. It can be used for military and banking operations, but its ciphers are not unbreakable. A scaled-down pocket version, called the "Lilliput," will soon be available for our regular subscribers.

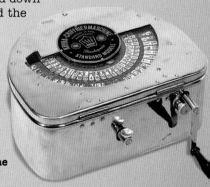

MC 0270 Kryha Machine
Includes spare handle

FREE! CAMOUFLAGE CARRYING CASE

M-209

This handy machine, developed by Swedish cryptographer Boris Hagelin, uses six movable alphabet rings to encrypt a message. The M-209 is durable, portable, and easy to operate. Very useful for brief battlefield messages.

CM 043 Cipher Machine Includes manual

SIGABA

Fifteen rotors enable this amazing World War II machine to create secure ciphertext. Plus, there is no record of its code being broken. Employed by the newly established NATO after the war, but no longer in use.

S 2310 Sigaba
Collector's item only

CD-57

Precision-made in Switzerland around 1957, the CD-57 is a hand-held mechanical cipher machine with six coding wheels. Its compact size made this device popular with the French Secret Service during the Cold War. Now available to members for a limited promotion.

CM 0000 CD 57 10% off for first-time buyers

ENIGMA

Best value! The German Enigma machine encrypts messages through its complex system of rotating scramblers. The German military relied on the Enigma during World War II. Provides a possible 10 quadrillion settings. Ingenious design and uncrackable—well, almost!

FREE! 750-PAGE INSTRUCTION MANUAL

S 1944 Enigma
Guaranteed delivery in 10 days

PRECISION-MADE IN CALIFORNIA

HEBERN ROTOR

Rookie American Edward Hebern built this cipher machine by connecting a pair of manual and electric typewriters to a letter-scrambling rotating device. His machine is among the earliest to use this rotor system, producing fiendishly difficult ciphertext.

CM 0070 Hebern Machine Will never rust

HEAVY ITEM—MUST BE PICKED UP IN PERSON

Tommy Flowers

COLOSSUS

This gigantic machine—Colossus—was built by British engineer Tommy Flowers in 1943. Its purpose was to supply possible settings to decrypt Enigma messages. With Colossus, messages can be cracked in hours rather than days. This machine could prove to be the forerunner to small computing devices, so get yours now!

CM 2011 Mega Machine Customer provides transportation

CODE BREAKING

Today's exam tests your skill at code breaking! Just as there are hundreds of codes and ciphers, there are many thousands of men and women busy taking a crack at them. The fancy name for code breaking is cryptanalysis and, to be a successful cryptanalyst, you need skill, determination, and patience. Computers can help crunch the numbers but only humans can do the big thinking and find the clues.

Black Chambers

In the 1700s, the best code breakers in Europe worked in secret offices known as Black Chambers—where diplomatic letters to embassies were intercepted. Working at top speed, code breakers copied out the coded letters before resealing them and sending them on. After cracking the codes, they passed the information to their superiors.

Exam 2:00 pm

Remember, early attempts at code breaking relied on frequency analysis—when certain letters appear more often than others. The most common letters in the English language are "E" and "T," while in German they are "T" and "A," and in Spanish "E" and "A." You can study the encoded text, see how often a particular letter appears, and then take a guess as to what it might be. Chalk one up for cryptanalysis!

EAO

ET A tas

Elizabethan plot

In the 16th century, Mary, Queen of Scots, plotted to have Elizabeth I murdered. Mary sent coded messages to her supporters, but the head of Elizabeth's secret service, Sir Francis Walsingham, intercepted them. Using frequency analysis, he deciphered the code and discovered the plot. Mary was executed in 1587.

Cipher success

For years, the Vigenère cipher was deemed unbreakable. Nevertheless, in the 1850s, British mathematician Charles Babbage decided to try his luck at cracking the cipher. He succeeded, but kept his secret to himself. Then, in 1863, a Prussian code breaker named Friedrich Kasiski wrote a booklet on how to break it and took the credit. Babbage later became a big wheel in computing.

Bombes away

During World War II, British math whiz Alan Turing worked for the Government Code and Cypher School. At its headquarters, Bletchley Park, Turing played a key role in deciphering the messages encrypted by the German Enigma machine, providing vital intelligence for the Allies. Turing's team designed a machine known as a bombe that could decode German messages.

Geek corner

Modern computers can create incredibly complicated codes—ones that can only be broken by even more powerful machines. Cipher codes that protect the security of huge networks, such as banking systems and the Internet, are now thought to be unbreakable. But history has taught us that there are ways to get around even the trickiest problems. Use your noggin, and you will log in.

Streng geheim

Secreto de Estado

Talking codes

Brilliant code breaker Agnes Driscoll joined the U.S. Navy in 1918. Her degree in math and physics, and fluency in languages, including Japanese, landed her a job on the cryptology team. Over a long career, "Miss Aggie" cracked one Japanese naval code after another through her determination and skill. She also worked on developing code-breaking machines and, for a time, was assigned to solve the Enigma machine code.

ENIGMA MACHINE

By the time World War II started, ever-more complex message-coding machines were swallowing secret information about military maneuvers and converting it into indecipherable ciphers. One device above all others proved frustratingly difficult to crack: the legendary Enigma machine. The Germans relied on the Enigma to direct U-boat submarine attacks on enemy ships. The most brilliant minds in Britain gathered at Bletchley Park to uncover the secret workings of the Enigma. Finally...jackpot!

PURPLE REIGN

Before entering the war, the Japanese built a cipher machine to encode messages in millions of combinations. The United States called the machine Purple (they kept its messages in purple files) and for a while it reigned supreme. But with the help of a replica, U.S. code breaker William Friedman unraveled its workings.

ENIGMA VARIATIONS

The German's secret weapon was the Enigma machine. Invented by Arthur Scherbius, the Enigma had a keyboard for typing in the message, a unit with up to eight spinning rotors to scramble it, and an illuminated lamp board to show each coded letter. There were eight trillion possible setting combinations.

POLES APART

Fearing a German invasion, Polish intelligence gave Marian Rejewski the challenge of cracking Enigma. He made good headway, but as Poland became less safe Rejewski handed his findings to British and French intelligence. The Germans then modified Enigma (and its codebook) to make it even more complex.

BEST OF BRITAIN

Back in Britain, the government recruited a crack team of mathematicians, scientists, chess champions, and engineers to unravel the secrets of Enigma. The team worked in numbered wooden huts built at Bletchley Park, known as Station X—the headquarters of British code-breaking activities.

HIT THE HUT

Code breakers worked eight hours on and eight hours off, all week. As the Enigma settings changed daily, new settings had to be discovered quickly. The huts were grouped in pairs. In one hut, workers cracked incoming ciphers; in the other, the deciphered messages were turned into intelligence reports.

THE BOMBE

Based on the Polish research, the British built the bombe, a device to help find the settings of the Enigma machine's rotors. The bombe eliminated wrong guesses, which was a huge time-saver. There were around 200 bombes at Bletchley and other backup stations, all working 24 hours a day.

HITTING THE JACKPOT!

One of the brightest minds at Bletchley was young mathematician Alan Turing. He figured out two major weaknesses in the Enigma, a line of thinking that eventually helped the team at Bletchley crack the code. Historians say that solving the puzzle shortened the war by two years, saving countless lives.

THE PERFECT CIPHER

CRACKING A 200-YEAR-OLD PRESIDENTIAL CODE

THE WHITE HOUSE, WASHINGTON, D.C. DECEMBER 1801. AMERICA'S THIRD PRESIDENT, THOMAS JEFFERSON, BURNS THE MIDNIGHT OIL IN HIS STUDY. AS THE PRINCIPAL AUTHOR OF THE DECLARATION OF INDEPENDENCE, JEFFERSON CERTAINLY HAD A WAY WITH WORDS, YET THE LETTER HE HAD JUST RECEIVED BAFFLED HIM.

WELL, I'LL BE VEXED. HE'S AS CLEVER AS A FOX.

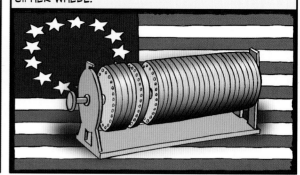

WHILE HE WAS AMERICA'S ENVOY TO FRANCE (1784–1789) AND GEORGE WASHINGTON'S SECRETARY OF STATE (1790–1793), JEFFERSON HAD RELIED ON SECRECY FOR SENSITIVE CORRESPONDENCE. A BRILLIANT INVENTOR, HE EVEN CREATED HIS OWN CIPHER WHEEL.

JEFFERSON'S FRIEND, ROBERT PATTERSON, WAS A MATH PROFESSOR AT THE UNIVERSITY OF PENNSYLVANIA. HE SHARED JEFFERSON'S FASCINATION WITH CODES AND CIPHERS, AND THE PAIR OFTEN WROTE LETTERS TO EACH OTHER AND MET TO DISCUSS THE MOST INGENIOUS CODES.

THIS CODE IS CHILD'S PLAY! IT'S SIMPLE TO LEARN, YES, AND EASY TO CRACK.

TOO TRUE, MR. PRESIDENT. THE BEST CODES MUST BE ABSOLUTELY INSCRUTABLE TO THOSE NOT IN ON THE SECRET.

I'VE GOT A CHALLENGE FOR YOU, MY FRIEND: CREATE THE PERFECT CODE. MAKE IT SO BRILLIANT IT BAFFLES THE BEST AND BRIGHTEST MINDS IN AMERICA.

I'LL TAKE THAT CHALLENGE. AND WHO WILL TRY TO CRACK IT?

NOW THAT IS A JOB FOR YOUR COMMANDER IN CHIEF!

SO PATTERSON TOOK THE CHALLENGE. WHEN HIS CIPHER WAS AS NEAR PERFECTION AS IT COULD GET, HE WROTE A LETTER TO JEFFERSON, INCLUDING A CODED PASSAGE.

THERE! I DEFY ANYONE—EVEN JEFFERSON—TO DECIPHER THIS.

NOBODY KNOWS WHETHER OR NOT JEFFERSON CRACKED THE CIPHER, ALTHOUGH HE MUST HAVE BEEN CONVINCED OF ITS EXCELLENCE, SINCE HE PASSED IT ALONG TO THE STATE DEPARTMENT. LATER, THE ENCIPHERED LETTER WAS FILED AWAY WITH JEFFERSON'S OTHER PRESIDENTIAL PAPERS, ITS MYSTERIOUS SECRET STILL LOCKED AWAY.

AROUND 200 YEARS LATER, DR. LAWREN SMITHLINE, A NEW JERSEY MATHEMATICIAN WHO DABBLES IN CODE BREAKING, HEARS THE STORY OF PATTERSON'S FLAWLESS CIPHER. HE OBTAINS A COPY OF THE LETTER AND GETS TO WORK. MANY SLEEPLESS NIGHTS FOLLOW...

THE CODE IS FIENDISHLY DIFFICULT. THE TEXT, CONTAINING NO CAPITAL LETTERS OR SPACES, CONSISTS OF 40 LINES OF AROUND 60 LETTERS EACH, BROKEN INTO SEEMINGLY RANDOM NUMBERED SECTIONS. RIGHT AWAY, SMITHLINE SEES THAT THIS IS NO SIMPLE CIPHER, WHERE ONE LETTER SUBSTITUTES FOR ANOTHER.

THERE MUST BE MILLIONS AND MILLIONS OF POSSIBLE COMBINATIONS TO SOLVE THIS.

PATTERSON'S LETTER EXPLAINED THAT THE KEY TO SOLVING THE CIPHER WAS KNOWING THE NUMBER OF LINES IN EACH SECTION OF TEXT, THE ORDER IN WHICH THEY FITTED, AND HOW MANY EXTRA LETTERS WERE ADDED ON.

I SEE. SO IF THE KEY IS 62, 51, I MOVE ROW 6 TO THE FIRST LINE OF A SECTION AND ADD TWO LETTERS. ROW 5 GOES TO THE SECOND LINE AND I ADD ONE LETTER.

SMITHLINE HAS A SUDDEN INSIGHT: HE DECIDES TO THINK IN PAIRS. IN ENGLISH, CERTAIN LETTER PAIRS (LIKE Q AND U) ALMOST ALWAYS GO TOGETHER, WHILE OTHERS NEVER APPEAR.

ALTHOUGH JEFFERSON'S USE OF ENGLISH WAS OLD-FASHIONED, SMITHLINE ANALYZES HIS STATE OF THE UNION ADDRESS AND TALLIES UP THE FREQUENCY OF LETTER PAIRS. THEN HE USES HIS EXPERIENCE TO APPLY A LITTLE GUESSWORK TO THE ORDERING OF THE TEXT SECTIONS.

JEFFERSON WAS AN AMAZINGLY GOOD WRITER, BUT MAN, THE WORDS PEOPLE USE HAVE CHANGED.

FOR A WEEK, SMITHLINE FOCUSES ON FINDING THE SOLUTION. HE HAS ONE 21ST-CENTURY ADVANTAGE: THE COMPUTER. HE TESTS HIS THEORIES AND ELIMINATES COUNTLESS POSSIBILITIES...

IMAGINE DOING THIS IN THE 19TH CENTURY! TEDIOUS BUT DOABLE. THANK YOU, COMPUTER!

AT LAST, THE NUMERICAL KEY EMERGES: 13, 34, 57, 65, 22, 78, 49.

YES!

SMITHLINE APPLIES THE KEY TO THE SCRAMBLED TEXT...

IN CONGRESS, JULY FOURTH, ONE THOUSAND SEVEN HUNDRED AND SEVENTY SIX... A DECLARATION BY THE REPRESENTATIVES OF THE UNITED STATES OF AMERICA...

WAIT A MINUTE! I'VE HEARD THIS BEFORE...

WHEN IN THE COURSE OF HUMAN EVENTS....

THE MESSAGE IS ALMOST EXACTLY THE SAME AS THE OPENING OF JEFFERSON'S FAMOUS DECLARATION OF INDEPENDENCE. PATTERSON HAD PLAYED A TRICK ON HIS OLD FRIEND, ENCRYPTING HIS OWN WORDS AND SENDING THEM BACK TO HIM.

SMITHLINE OUTFOXED THE CIPHER AND SOLVED A 200-YEAR-OLD PUZZLE. HE IS NOW A PROFESSIONAL CODE BREAKER.

WE'VE GOT A NEW CIPHER TO SOLVE FROM THE DEFENSE DEPARTMENT. IT LOOKS LIKE A DOOZY. WHO WANTS TO DO IT? HEADS OR TAILS?

HEADS!

HEADS IT IS...

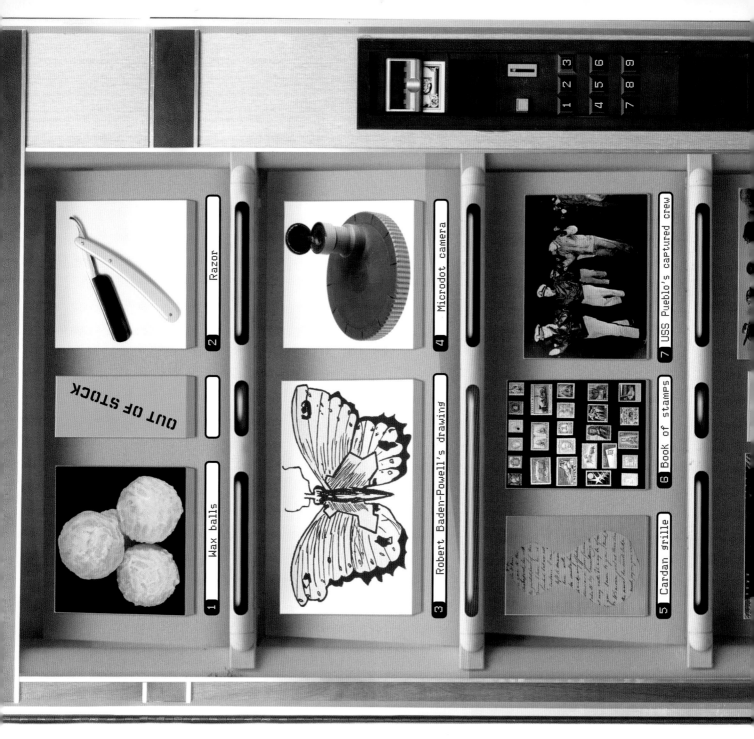

OUT OF STOCK

1 Wax balls

2 Razor

3 Robert Baden-Powell's drawing

4 Microdot camera

5 Cardan grille

6 Book of stamps

7 USS Pueblo's captured crew

① WAX WORKS

The ancient Chinese had a unique method of sending secret messages. They would write them on pieces of silk and encase them in balls of wax. A messenger would then swallow the wax balls and carry them in his stomach to their destination. The unfortunate recipient would then have to wait for nature to take its course!

② A CLOSE SHAVE

An ancient Greek king came up with this harebrained scheme: He shaved the head of his most trusted slave and tattooed a message on the unfortunate fellow's scalp. After the hair grew back and covered the message, the slave was sent to deliver the message, which was revealed by shaving his head once again.

③ WINGING IT

While working as a scout for the British Army, Lord Robert Baden-Powell would sketch intricate images of butterflies, but instead of drawing the real markings of the butterfly's wings, he would draw plans of enemy artillery positions. No one would guess that his butterflies were butter-spies.

④ SPOT THE DOTS

The invention of photography allowed spies to come up with all kinds of flashy ideas for passing information. During both world wars, German spies would photograph a secret message and then shrink it down to a dot the size of a period. The "microdots" were then hidden in the text of a magazine or newspaper.

⑤ FULL OF HOLES

Some methods of steganography are very complicated, others are wholly different. The Cardan grille is very simple indeed—just a piece of paper with holes cut into it. A message is hidden within a large piece of text, and when the grille is placed over the top of it, only the message is visible through the holes.

HIDDEN MESSAGES

At some point a spy is going to have to send all the information he has gathered back to his bosses. But he can't just slip it in an envelope marked "please don't read this, it's secret"—a spy needs to be more cunning. Steganography is the art of hiding a message in plain sight—it might be hidden behind a stamp or in someone's sweater, but you have to know where to look...

6 STAMP OF APPROVAL

When it comes to simplicity, this one has them all licked! This technique involves writing your message on the back of a postage stamp, sticking it on to a letter, and then mailing it. This obviously only works if your letter arrives in time...

7 SAY CHEESE!

When the American ship USS *Pueblo* was captured by North Korea in 1968, the crew was forced by the enemy captors to pose for propaganda photos. But the crew had a handy way to get a message back home: In the photos they placed their fingers in seemingly innocent positions, but they were actually sending a message!

8 A GOOD YARN

Why not get your grandma to use her knitting skills for a little spying? She could knit a secret message into an item of clothing or perhaps even a rug. The message could be hidden on a single thread, or stitched into the design in the form of pictograms.

9 SHE'S A DOLL

Sometimes it's best to keep it simple: Why use microfilm when a code word will suffice? Velvalee Dickinson spied for the Japanese in New York. She owned a doll shop and thus had good reason to be sending letters about dolls. However, when she wrote of three "dolls" coming from New York, she actually meant warships!

GOING DIGITAL!

In the age of social networking you can connect with your friends instantly. Spies, too, can take advantage of new technology to communicate with each other. They conceal messages in the 1s and 0s—the binary code—that make up digital files. This sophisticated science is known as digital steganography and it enables spies to correspond in ways that are almost impossible to detect.

CARRIED AWAY

Digital steganography is used in image and text files, sound and video files, and HTML (the language of web pages). These familiar "carriers" can transport hidden data without ever attracting attention. It's almost impossible to look at a carrier, like a photo of a cat or an MP3 file, and figure out that two people are using it to communicate in secret. Digital steganography not only keeps people from discovering the information—it prevents them from knowing it even exists.

COVERT COMMUNICATION

The basic practice of going digital is the same, no matter what type of file is used to carry the message, and because digital files are so large, they are the perfect medium in which to embed secret messages. Today, there are hundreds of computer programs that can identify the unimportant parts of a file and replace those parts with the secret message. In this way, the sender tampers with the data so slightly that the changes are not obvious. Once altered, the file is called a stego.

HOW IT WORKS

Hidden in plain sight on the Internet, the stego must reach its destination without its confidential message being garbled, destroyed, or discovered. At the receiving end, the intended recipient must know how to extract its secrets, known as the payload. There may be an agreed-upon key to ensure the message is retrieved.

PIXELS IN PHOTOS

Photographic files, such as JPEGs, are one of the most common carriers. To hide a message in a photo, the sender can tinker with the pixels (the colored dots that make up a digital photo). After removing the least important parts of a pixel and replacing them with a secret message, the photo will look the same to an untrained eye. The stego file can then be e-mailed, or posted on a social networking or photo-sharing site, where an accomplice can download it and retrieve the message. Intelligence agencies now use software to scan images for signs of tampering.

LOST IN MUSIC

The method is the same with digital audio files: Conceal the hidden message in the carrier while avoiding any noticeable changes in the quality of the sound. Sound files may contain stego messages in the least significant parts of the data—in the lowest parts of a noisy file, for example.

HIDDEN IN VIDEO

Pictures and messages can be concealed within video files. Random frames or parts of the picture on several frames are replaced with secret data. The small changes are not visible to the human eye when the video is replayed, but the recipient may slow it down or speed it up to retrieve the payload.

COVERED IN SNOW

Secrets can be hidden in text documents or e-mails through a method called snow. This software hides messages in the white spaces that occur between words and lines. Information can be concealed within "tweets" or on other social networks. Software inventors say that this helps people communicate in countries where governments control Internet use. There are also sneaky ways to send messages by "piggybacking" them onto normal Internet traffic.

IDLE CHITCHAT

For every new technology that we invent, steganographers come up with inventive ways to exploit it. Messages can hide within the data stream of VoIP (Voice over Internet Protocol) phone calls. VoIP is a method of turning sounds, such as a conversation, into digital data that can travel via the Internet. Secret messages can be squeezed between the packets of data that are carrying a caller's voice.

SECURITY SOFTWARE

Digital steganography can be close to foolproof. Despite the millions of dollars that are reportedly invested in global electronic eavesdropping systems and "sniffing" software, the sheer volume of Internet traffic makes hidden messages difficult to detect. The latest security software is designed to alert Internet users to any suspicious communication rather than crack the digital codes. As technology improves, security experts hope for a breakthrough, and some spies will find that their number is up!

SECRET WRITING

In addition to using codes, spies may communicate by writing messages that remain invisible until exposed to heat or light, or washed in a chemical bath. These documents reveal nothing if they fall into enemy hands, but the right person will know how to make the writing visible and uncover the message. An invisible message could be written in the space between each sentence of a letter so that only the clued-in or cunning could read between the lines.

LEMON JUICE • SWEAT • SALIVA • MILK

WHITE INK • SECRET INGREDIENT

Strange brew

Many everyday liquids double as invisible "inks" for sending messages, from lemon juice, cola, and milk to sweat, saliva, and urine. These acidic substances leave a residue behind when they dry. Then, when the paper is heated over a light bulb or a candle, the residue darkens and the message becomes visible.

White ink

Invisible inks can also be created with chemicals. During the American Revolution, George Washington's spies relied on "white ink" to exchange confidential information about British troops. With one chemical for writing messages and a second one for making them appear, white ink offered a double dose of detection prevention.

Smart stationery

During World War II, German prisoners held in the United States and Canada were given glossy postcards or paper for their letters home. The smooth paper was less likely to soak up invisible-ink messages. Another preventive measure used paper ruled with ink that bled if watery invisible ink was applied.

Musical notes

Hiding invisible writing on a printed document provides extra cover. During World War I, German entertainer Courtney de Rysbach toured Britain, collecting applause as well as secret information. He sent messages to his spymasters written in invisible ink on his sheet music, but in 1915 he was caught by MI5 and forced to face the music.

THE LADDER OF LOVE.

Chemistry set

The East German Stasi (secret police) used a clever method to send secret messages during the Cold War. Two sheets of plain paper sandwiched a third sheet coated with chemicals. As an agent wrote on the top sheet, the chemical transferred to the bottom sheet. Dunking the paper in a chemical mix made the message appear.

MANGANESE SULFATE

HYDROGEN PEROXIDE

PARTY MIX

Nushu writing

Until the 20th century, girls in China were forbidden to go to school. To educate themselves, women invented a language called Nushu, which they wrote in books and on fans. During the Japanese takeover of the 1940s, Nushu was banned to prevent the Chinese from using it for secret messages.

Carbon copies

The CIA adapted carbon-paper copying by creating special paper backed with invisible chemicals. This paper was put on top of a blank sheet of paper. When it was written on, the pressure from the pen transferred chemicals to the bottom sheet to duplicate the message. The receiving agent used water or heat to make the message visible.

SPYWARE

What gadgets and gizmos do top spies have hidden in their trench coats (or their shoes or pens)? From bullet-firing lipstick to picture-taking contact lenses, the range of devices will leave you shaken and stirred. Is something bugging you? Check out your gadgets. With spyware technology on laptops and phones, you never know who might be listening in.

WHAT'S WATCHING YOU?

Spies rely on lots of nifty devices to keep a close eye on their targets. A mission that involves spying on a suspect, keeping a close eye on a building, or tailing someone in the dark is going to require some very special equipment. Most importantly, a device shouldn't give a spy away, so the devices are often very small or subtly disguised in everyday objects, from plant pots and buttons to teddy bears and toothbrushes. So which of the items opposite could be watching you?

EARLY DEVICES

The earliest cameras were big and bulky, but the Super Subminiature Box Camera, made in the 1870s, changed all that. It was 2.7 in (7 cm) high and easily hidden inside a pocket. The cunningly disguised Tica Expo Watch Camera, first made in 1905, was even smaller at just 2.1 in (5.4 cm) wide.

GETTING SMALLER

In the 1930s, the French Lumière brothers created the mini Eljy camera. At a mere 3 in (7.6 cm) across, it was still a giant compared to the American Petal Camera of the 1940s. The Petal was about the size and shape of a coin, and thus fitted easily in the palm of the hand.

THE MUST-HAVE

The Minox became the standard camera for intelligence agencies from World War II to the 1980s. Palm-sized and lightweight, it was often used for photographing documents. James Bond even used one in the 1967 film *You Only Live Twice*.

PART OF THE ATTIRE

During the Cold War, spies hid cameras on themseves using devices like the German Steinbeck ABC wristwatch camera. The CIA and KGB also both used "coat button cameras," which were disguised as buttons and operated by a lever in the coat pocket.

GOING DIGITAL

Digital technology in the 1990s revolutionized spy cameras. Digital cameras can take very sharp images and are so small that they can be hidden in almost anything. In fact, the PI-Camcorder Tiny Tek Stick fits inside a package of chewing gum.

COPYCAT CAMERAS

In the 1960s, the KGB developed a camera that looked like a normal leather wallet, for secretly copying documents. Today, secret digital mini-scanners can scan hundreds of files while looking like innocent credit cards, pens, and other objects.

LONG-DISTANCE VISION

Telescopes and binoculars have let spies spy from afar ever since the 17th century. Binoculars are good for surveillance work since they can be held steadily in the hands, while a monocular (single lens) is small enough to hide on you at all times.

SEEING IN THE DARK

When darkness falls, a spy can resort to night-vision goggles. They gather and amplify small amounts of light, allowing the wearer to see in the dark. If there is no light at all, spies can use a thermal imager, which registers the heat given off by people.

Top of the taps

The phone tap—a device used to secretly listen in on telephone conversations—is one of the oldest forms of audio surveillance. Technological advances over the years have made tapping much easier. Taps no longer have to be attached to the target's telephone system, but can be monitored by computer from the phone company's central network instead.

Tunnel tap

Tapping hasn't always been easy. In the 1950s, the United States and Britain dug a tunnel under Berlin, East Germany, to access the Soviet Union's phone lines. The Soviets were expecting them, however, having been tipped off by a mole working for MI6. To protect their mole, they let the tap go ahead for 11 months before finally "discovering" it.

Czech your shoes

The U.S. ambassador to Czechoslovakia ordered some shoes by mail order in the 1960s. The Czech secret police intercepted the package and planted bugs in the heels, allowing them to listen to the ambassador's conversations wherever he went.

ALL EARS

Finding out what the enemy is talking about is one of the main goals of spying. Once upon a time, spies had to creep up on their targets to eavesdrop on their conversations, which could be dangerous. Today's spies can listen in from far away by using hidden bugs, tapping into phone calls, or turning cell phones into secret listening devices.

Stumped!

Bugs can be concealed almost anywhere. In the 1970s, the United States planted one inside a fake tree stump in Moscow, using it to intercept communications coming from a nearby Soviet air base. The bug was solar-powered, so spies didn't need to reveal it, or themselves, to change its batteries. Despite this, the Russians eventually discovered and disabled it.

Going buggy

A bug consists of a tiny microphone for recording sound, and a tiny radio transmitter for relaying that sound to the spy's receiving equipment. The receiving equipment is usually hidden some distance away, perhaps in an unremarkable vehicle that won't stand out, parked outside the target's home.

Bug in your drink

To show just how far bugging technology had come by the 1960s, an American private detective, Hal Lipset, demonstrated a bugging device hidden inside a fake olive floating in a drink. It had a toothpick for an antenna and a listening range of 30 ft (9 m).

Spy kids

The Soviets came up with a cunning plan for bugging the U.S. embassy in Moscow in 1945: They got local schoolchildren to present the U.S. ambassador to the Soviet Union with a wooden replica of the Great Seal of the United States. He gratefully accepted the gift, not realizing that Soviet spies had placed a bug inside, which they used to eavesdrop on the embassy for six years before it was discovered.

Mobile microphones

Many governments insist that cell phone companies equip each phone with software that allows the phone's internal microphone to be switched on, turning it into a bug. The clever part is that it can be done without turning on the phone itself, so the owner doesn't realize that they're being listened to.

Crawling with bugs

The Great Seal bug was child's play compared to what happened in the 1980s. When the Soviets built the United States a brand-new embassy in Moscow, it turned out to have so many Soviet bugs that the U.S. had to demolish part of it in 1985 before they had even moved in. Two replacement bug-free floors, built by the U.S., were opened in 2000.

Catching bugs

Every intelligence agency spends as much time making sure their own side isn't being bugged as they do bugging the enemy. They scan sensitive government buildings using electronic detectors, which pick up radio waves given out by bugs. However, some bugs operate only at certain times, making them harder to detect. X-ray machines may be used to find these.

Planting a bug

Bugs have to be hidden so the target doesn't realize they're being monitored. Some are planted in the target's home or office, in places they wouldn't think to look for them, such as in a clock or behind a picture. Others are carried by spies and disguised as everyday objects, such as pens or watches.

GADGETS AND GIZMOS

In almost every James Bond movie, agent "Q" gives Bond a bizarre gadget, such as a watch with a laser-beam cutting tool, a credit card with X-ray capabilities, or an invisible car. Real intelligence agencies may not have perfected any of these gadgets yet, but they've certainly come up with some equally ingenious devices.

CRAFTY CARDS

There was a real-life equivalent of "Q" named Charles Fraser-Smith. He worked for MI6 during World War II, creating amazing spy gadgets such as saws hidden inside hairbrushes, knives placed in the soles of shoes, and maps concealed inside playing cards.

SECRET CHAMBERS

In World War II, Britain's chief sabotage organization, the SOE (Special Operations Executive), produced lots of inventive spy gear, including very realistic-looking plaster logs filled with weapons, and toothpaste tubes with secret chambers for hiding objects such as maps or tools.

TWO-IN-ONE PANTS BUTTONS

Many SOE gadgets were cunningly disguised as everyday objects. Spies who got lost could find their way by removing their special pants buttons: Balanced on top of each other, the buttons would act like a compass, pointing north.

STEALTHY SNEAKERS

The SOE also gave British soldiers special shoes to disguise their presence when they arrived on the sandy shores of southeast Asia. The soles of the shoes were designed to leave harmless-looking bare footprints rather than heavy boot prints, which would have given them away to the enemy.

BOOBY-TRAPPED BRIEFCASE

To protect secret documents, the SOE invented a special briefcase. Only British spies knew that, to open it, they had to push the right-hand button down and to the right. If the enemy found the case and used the left-hand button, the case would explode, destroying its secret contents.

GETAWAY BIKE

One of the SOE's most successful devices was the Welbike: This miniature folding motorcycle could be dropped behind enemy lines by parachute, and then assembled by a spy in a matter of seconds. More than 3,000 were made.

CUNNING CANOE

A cross between a canoe and a submarine, this device was used by British spies during World War II to plant bombs next to enemy ships. It could operate both on the surface and underwater, where the pilot would breathe through scuba gear.

ELECTRONIC ROCK

In 2006, the Russian government accused British spies of using a fake rock planted on a Moscow street to pass messages to one another. The rock was equipped with electronic equipment so that the spies could upload and download data to it using their cell phones.

GLOBAL EAVESDROPPING

Every day, billions of electronic signals are sent whizzing around the world as phone calls, e-mails, radar transmissions, and text messages.

Governments can check for threats against national security by gathering up as many of these signals as they can. But then comes the difficult part: separating the useful intelligence from the mass of irrelevant communication.

Data collection

Electronic information is collected in a number of ways. Hardware devices and software programs monitor communication networks and record the content of phone calls, e-mails, and web traffic. Many governments insist that telephone companies make sure that their networks can be easily tapped by security agencies, if required. In addition, huge radio antennae act like giant vacuum cleaners, sucking up enormous amounts of radio signals and satellite transmissions.

Supercomputers

Just collecting vast amounts of information isn't very useful—it all needs to be analyzed. The enormous pile of data hits a funneling system and powerful supercomputers sift through all the signals to find the important stuff for agents to focus on. The National Security Agency (NSA) in the United States is said to own the world's largest group of supercomputers, and to employ the most math whizzes of any organization, to help with the analysis and code breaking.

SIGINT

Signals intelligence (SIGINT) is the lingo used by those in the know for the whole process by which signals are collected, decrypted, and analyzed. The supercomputers use special programs that "data mine" the information, carefully scanning it to pick out the potentially useful parts and discarding the rest. The human analysts can then focus their attention on the relevant signals to pull out any nuggets of valuable intelligence.

ELINT

The part of SIGINT that deals with the general collection and analysis of signals that are sent between electronic devices is known as ELINT (electronics intelligence). ELINT often involves tracking the signals that are sent out by enemy radar, ships, aircraft, missile systems, and other military equipment.

COMINT

The part of SIGINT that deals with the collection and analysis of electronic messages that are sent between people is known as COMINT (communications intelligence). This includes both voice communication, such as radio transmissions and phone conversations, and written communication in the form of e-mails and texts.

Menwith Hill

With 30 giant ball-shaped antennae, known as radomes, Menwith Hill in England is said to be the center of Project Echelon and is one of the world's biggest electronic monitoring stations. It is apparently capable of gathering millions of signals an hour, which are relayed to the project's SIGINT agencies.

Project Echelon

Founded just after World War II by the United States and Britain to spy on the Soviets, the UKUSA agreement, known as Project Echelon, is run largely in secret but now involves Canada, Australia, and New Zealand, too. Believed to be the world's largest signals intelligence operation, it plays a major part in counterterrorism.

SIGINT agencies

Every government has an organization in charge of signals intelligence. The NSA operates in the United States, while China's Third Department runs an ever-growing SIGINT operation across Asia. Russia is also said to maintain a large global spying presence through its network of antennae and satellites.

SATELLITE SURVEILLANCE

Since the late 1950s, hundreds of satellites have been launched into orbit around Earth. Many are used for communications and television broadcasts, but some have a more sinister application. From their vantage point high in space, they can be used by governments to spy on other countries, transmitting images and messages back to the operator in an instant via radio signals.

Spy satellites

All of the world's leading powers, including the United States, Russia, and China, operate spy satellites. Some satellites eavesdrop on communications, others intercept electronic signals, and still others take high-definition photographs of targets down on Earth.

Long drop

The first American spy satellites were launched as part of the Corona program (1959–1972). They had cameras that could focus down on objects that were 25 ft (7.5 m) wide on Earth. The photos were taken using film that had to be developed on Earth, so capsules containing the film were dropped back into Earth's atmosphere and caught by American planes.

Astro spies

In the 1960s and 1970s, the United States and the Soviet Union both experimented with manned satellites. Each developed its own program, but the idea was the same for both: Spacecraft would be fired into orbit, where astronauts equipped with telescopes and cameras would gaze down on the enemy. Both projects arrived at the same conclusion—they were too expensive to operate—so both were abandoned.

Overhead eavesdropper

Since the 1960s, the United States has been operating SIGINT (signals intelligence) satellites. These robotic spies in space tap into the military and diplomatic communications of other countries by intercepting electronic communications, such as radar and radio messages. Each SIGINT satellite is believed to cost in the region of $1 billion.

Spotted at sea

American satellites track military targets at sea, gathering ELINT (electronic intelligence) on warships, missiles, and submarines. The National Ocean Surveillance System uses groups of three satellites, which, operating together, can precisely locate their targets. The system was begun in the 1970s to spy on the Soviet fleet and is still used today to identify terrorist and criminal targets.

All-seeing eye

An observation satellite is like a giant telescope, but one that is pointed at Earth rather than outer space. Today's most powerful satellites can see objects just 5 in (12 cm) wide on the surface of the planet. However, these satellites are constantly orbiting Earth, so they are unable to hover directly over their targets for long.

Now you see it...

The recent development of antisatellite weapons has prompted countries to develop "invisible" or stealth satellites. Some experts believe that the United States has been working on a cloaking device to prevent its satellites from being picked up by cameras or radar. However, not much is known about this—not only is the program classified, but if the device works properly, we will never know!

Follow that car!

GPS (Global Positioning System) is a navigational tool operated by the United States government. Anyone on Earth with a GPS receiver can find their position by communicating with navigational satellites. However, the GPS system can also be used by spies down here on Earth, who can secretly attach a GPS tracking device to a vehicle to track a target's movements.

HACK JOB

Secretly breaking into a computer or a computer system is called hacking. Hackers do this for many reasons, both good and bad. They may want to steal data, snoop on competitors, or sometimes just test the security of a computer system so that it can be improved. They use an array of techniques to get past computer security systems—such as password cracking, packet sniffing, and vulnerability scanning—but all have the same ultimate goal: to reveal information that is usually off-limits.

① White hats
"Good" hackers who work with the permission of the computer system's owner are called white hats. They are often hired to test the system to see how easy it would be for a "bad" hacker to break into it.

② Black hats
People hacking without the permission of the computer system's owner are known as black hats. They may aim to steal useful information, or damage a rival's research, but sometimes they hack just for the challenge.

③ Gray hats
Gray hats hack without permission, but instead of doing damage, they inform the owners that they have broken through their security, giving them the chance to fix the problem (or offering to fix it themselves for a fee).

④ Hacktivists
Hacktivists break into computer systems for political or moral reasons. In 2010, hactivist supporters of the whistle-blowing website Wikileaks launched cyber attacks against credit card companies who had withdrawn their services from Wikileaks.

⑤ Password cracking
One of the most common ways that hackers break into computer systems is by cracking passwords. This can involve everything from stealing an employee's password to using programs that "guess" a password by trying every possible combination. The latter is known as the brute-force method and requires extremely powerful computers that can try billions of possible combinations per second.

6 Installing spyware

People can be tricked into installing programs on their computers that secretly record information. This can be done by "baiting"—leaving a USB stick that looks like it contains exciting contents somewhere where the target will find it.

7 War dialing

To find computers to break into, hackers can "war dial" them. This involves using a modem to call all the phone numbers in an area to find out which ones are answered by a computer. The hacker can then attempt to crack those computers.

8 Spoofing

The computer hacker's equivalent of a false mustache, glasses, and hat, spoofing is when a malicious program is disguised as a nice, friendly one, sending false data to a target computer to trick it into letting the hacker gain access to classified information.

9 Social engineering

Hackers often try to social-engineer, or trick, employees into revealing information about their organization's computer security. They may do this by making friends with the employee, by phoning them and pretending to be a coworker, or by "phishing"—sending a bogus "official" e-mail requesting security information.

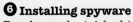

10 Vulnerability scanning

Using special computer programs to find weaknesses in a computer system's security that hackers can exploit is called vulnerability scanning. It's similar to how a conventional spy might look for an open back door or an unlocked window to gain entry to a building.

11 Packet sniffing

The computer hacker's equivalent of a phone tap, a packet sniffer is a device used to intercept digital traffic being sent between computers on a network, including e-mails, website information, and passwords. It gets its name from the fact that, when data is sent between computers, it is broken down into small chunks known as "packets."

12 Phreaking out

Telephone companies once used certain sounds, or tones, to control their calls. Some people discovered that blowing a tuned whistle into the receiver enabled them to place free long-distance calls. However, this practice, called phreaking, died out when telephone systems became digital. That blew it for phreakers.

FREE SOFTWARE

Hello?

Hello!

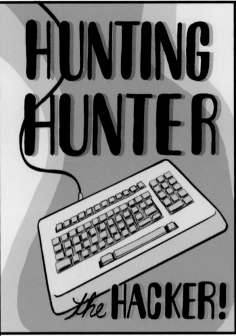

HUNTING HUNTER
the HACKER!

IN 1986, AMERICAN CLIFFORD STOLL MANAGED A NETWORK OF COMPUTERS AT THE LAWRENCE BERKELEY NATIONAL LABORATORY (LBNL) IN CALIFORNIA. THE LAB HAD SET UP AN ACCOUNTING PROGRAM THAT CHARGED THE USER WHEN A COMPUTER WAS USED. ONE DAY, CLIFF'S BOSS NOTICED A PROBLEM.

LBNL COMPUTER LAB

CLIFF, CAN I SPEAK TO YOU FOR A MINUTE?

SURE, WHAT IS IT?

CLIFF'S BOSS HAD NOTICED AN ERROR IN THE AUTOMATED ACCOUNTS. THERE WAS 75 CENTS OF COMPUTER TIME THAT HADN'T BEEN PAID FOR. ALTHOUGH IT WAS ONLY A SMALL AMOUNT OF MONEY, THE PROGRAM WAS NOT WRONG, SO HE ASKED CLIFF TO INVESTIGATE.

I'M SURE IT'S NOTHING SERIOUS, BUT COULD YOU LOOK INTO THIS MISSING 75 CENTS FOR ME?

PAID
PAID
PAID
PAID
PAID
PAID

OUTSTANDING $0.75

NO PROBLEM.

CLIFF SOON FOUND THAT THE MISSING 75 CENTS WORTH OF COMPUTER TIME HAD BEEN RACKED UP BY A USER WITH THE LOG-IN "HUNTER." BUT THERE WASN'T A "HUNTER" WORKING AT THE LAB. SO WHO COULD IT BE?

WELL, HE'S NOT ONE OF US.

CLIFF DISCOVERED THAT "HUNTER" WAS A HACKER WHO HAD GAINED ACCESS TO THE NETWORK FROM OUTSIDE THE LAB. HE USED A "SYSTEM MANAGER" ACCOUNT, WHICH MEANT HE HAD TOTAL ACCESS TO THE NETWORK AND COULD CHANGE INFORMATION ON IT.

CLIFF DETERMINED THAT HUNTER WAS ACCESSING THE NETWORK VIA A TELEPHONE MODEM CONNECTION, USING ONE OF THE LAB'S FIVE HIGH-SPEED PHONE LINES. BUT WHICH ONE? TO FIND OUT, CLIFF CONNECTED A COMPUTER TO EACH OF THE FIVE LINES.

GOT HIM!

WHEN THE HACKER CONNECTED, THE RELEVANT COMPUTER STARTED PRINTING A REPORT, LETTING CLIFF KNOW WHICH PHONE LINE HE WAS USING.

NOW THAT HE HAD IDENTIFIED THE SOURCE, CLIFF BEGAN MONITORING THE HACKER'S ACTIVITIES TO FIGURE OUT WHAT HE WAS AFTER.

BEEP! BEEP!

TO MAKE SURE HE DIDN'T MISS ANYTHING, CLIFF BEGAN SLEEPING IN THE LAB UNDER HIS DESK. HE PROGRAMMED HIS PAGER TO BEEP WHENEVER THE HACKER CAME ONLINE.

CLIFF PROGRAMMED THE COMPUTER TO PRINT OUT THE HACKER'S KEYSTROKES. BY READING THESE PRINTOUTS, HE COULD SEE HUNTER'S MOVES ONLINE.

HMM...THIS MIGHT TAKE A WHILE.

CLIFF NOTICED THAT THE HACKER MOSTLY CAME ONLINE IN THE MIDDLE OF THE DAY, WHICH SEEMED STRANGE SINCE THIS WAS WHEN PHONE CALLS WERE MOST EXPENSIVE. HE REALIZED THAT THE HACKER MUST BE IN A FOREIGN COUNTRY, AND WAS PHONING WHEN IT WAS NIGHTTIME WHERE HE WAS AND CALLS WERE CHEAPER.

ALWAYS AT THE SAME TIME... THE GUY MUST BE PHONING FROM ABROAD.

BUT WHERE FROM?

CLIFF DECIDED TO CALL THE FBI TO TELL THEM WHAT HE'D FOUND. BUT THEY DIDN'T SEEM THAT INTERESTED.

I THINK YOU SHOULD LOOK INTO THIS.

IT'S ONLY 75 CENTS. IT'S NOT EXACTLY CRIME OF THE CENTURY.

DESPITE THE FBI'S LACK OF INTEREST, CLIFF KEPT ON INVESTIGATING. HE WANTED TO KNOW EXACTLY WHAT THE HACKER WAS DOING. GRADUALLY IT BECAME CLEAR THAT THE HACKER WAS USING THE LBNL NETWORK TO GAIN ACCESS TO OTHER NETWORKS, ESPECIALLY MILITARY BASES, WHERE HE WOULD PERFORM SEARCHES FOR WORDS SUCH AS "NUCLEAR" AND "SDI" (STRATEGIC DEFENSE INITIATIVE).

POOR SECURITY WAS TO BLAME FOR HUNTER'S SUCCESS IN BREAKING INTO THE NETWORKS. IN THE EARLY DAYS OF THE INTERNET, PEOPLE WERE LESS AWARE OF THE IMPORTANCE OF PASSWORDS THAN THEY ARE NOW. MANY LEFT THEM BLANK OR USED DEFAULT ONES, SUCH AS "1234," WHICH WERE EASY TO GUESS. THIS WAS TRUE EVEN AT MANY MILITARY BASES, MUCH TO CLIFF'S ASTONISHMENT.

WHOA, THIS IS SERIOUS. THIS GUY IS SOME KIND OF SPY!!

PASSWORD: 1234 accepted

WE'RE DEFENSELESS!

THE HACKER WAS LOOKING FOR MILITARY SECRETS.

WITH THE HELP OF OTHER COMPUTER AND TELEPHONE EXPERTS, CLIFF WAS ABLE TO TRACE THE HACKER TO GERMANY, WHERE HE WAS CALLING USING A SATELLITE LINK. BUT HUNTER WAS NEVER ONLINE LONG ENOUGH TO BE TRACED DIRECTLY.

CLIFF CONTACTED THE FBI AGAIN AND TOLD THEM WHAT HE KNEW. WHEN THEY REALIZED MILITARY SECRETS WERE INVOLVED, AND THAT THE HACKER WAS A FOREIGNER, THE FBI WAS SUDDENLY MUCH MORE INTERESTED.

CLIFF'S GIRLFRIEND CAME UP WITH AN IDEA OF HOW TO KEEP HUNTER ONLINE LONG ENOUGH FOR HIM TO BE CAUGHT—BY PLANTING A "HONEYPOT" OF IMPORTANT-SOUNDING (BUT FAKE) MILITARY SECRETS ON THE COMPUTER SYSTEM, WHICH WOULD ATTRACT THE HACKER, BUT WOULD ALSO TAKE SEVERAL HOURS TO DOWNLOAD.

SHOOT! WE ALMOST GOT HIM THAT TIME!

THIS GUY'S STEALING MILITARY SECRETS.

WE'LL BE RIGHT OVER!

IF IT'S MILITARY SECRETS HE WANTS, WHY DON'T YOU MAKE SOME UP?

THAT'S A GREAT IDEA.

THE PLOY WORKED. THE HACKER TOOK THE BAIT AND STAYED ONLINE LONG ENOUGH FOR THE FBI TO CONTACT THE GERMAN AUTHORITIES, AND FOR THEM TO TRACK HIM DOWN AT HIS HOME IN HANOVER, GERMANY.

THE HACKER'S NAME WAS MARKUS HESS, AND HE'D BEEN STEALING MILITARY SECRETS AND SELLING THEM TO THE RUSSIAN SECRET SERVICE, THE KGB, FOR YEARS.

CLIFF, ON THE OTHER HAND, WENT ON TO WRITE A BEST-SELLING BOOK ABOUT HIS EXPERIENCE SAVING AMERICA'S MILITARY SECRETS AND SUCCESSFULY HUNTING THE HACKER.

THESE ARE GREAT SECRETS!

YOU ARE UNDER ARREST FOR INTERNATIONAL ESPIONAGE.

CRIME DOESN'T PAY.

HESS WAS SENT TO JAIL FOR TWO YEARS FOR HIS CRIMES.

"HUNTER" BECAME THE HUNTED!

SPIES IN THE SKY

Almost as soon as flying machines were invented, they were drafted into spying missions. Particularly useful during times of war, they give spies eyes in the sky to get a better look at the enemy's numbers, weapons, and movements. Since they first took to the skies in the 20th century, airplanes have been the main flying reconnaissance vehicles, and spy planes have been among the fastest and highest-flying aircraft ever built.

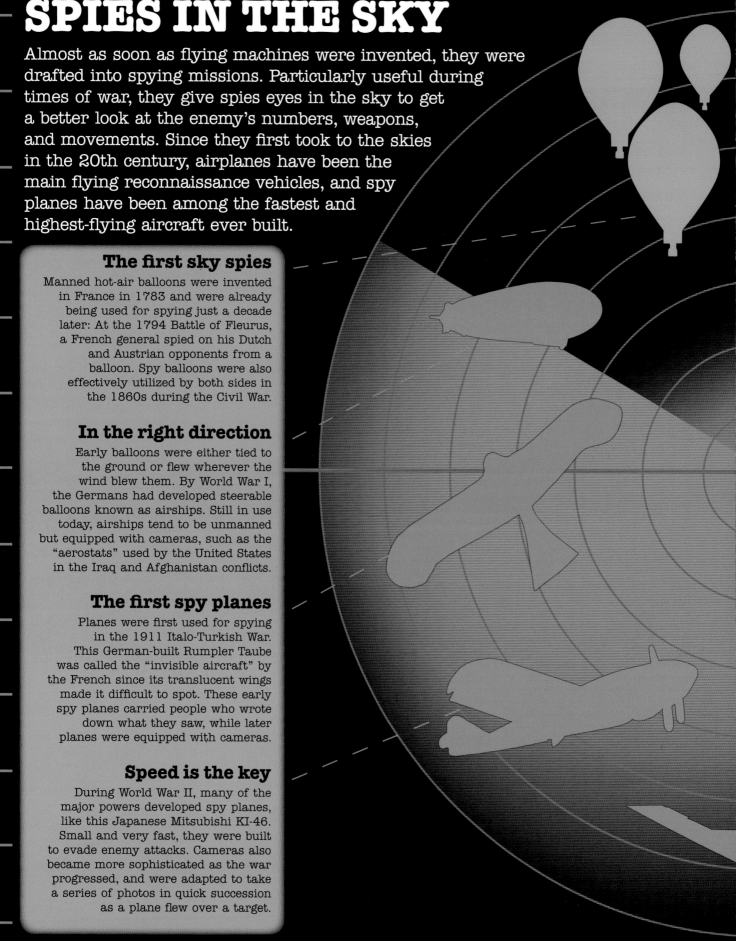

The first sky spies

Manned hot-air balloons were invented in France in 1783 and were already being used for spying just a decade later: At the 1794 Battle of Fleurus, a French general spied on his Dutch and Austrian opponents from a balloon. Spy balloons were also effectively utilized by both sides in the 1860s during the Civil War.

In the right direction

Early balloons were either tied to the ground or flew wherever the wind blew them. By World War I, the Germans had developed steerable balloons known as airships. Still in use today, airships tend to be unmanned but equipped with cameras, such as the "aerostats" used by the United States in the Iraq and Afghanistan conflicts.

The first spy planes

Planes were first used for spying in the 1911 Italo-Turkish War. This German-built Rumpler Taube was called the "invisible aircraft" by the French since its translucent wings made it difficult to spot. These early spy planes carried people who wrote down what they saw, while later planes were equipped with cameras.

Speed is the key

During World War II, many of the major powers developed spy planes, like this Japanese Mitsubishi KI-46. Small and very fast, they were built to evade enemy attacks. Cameras also became more sophisticated as the war progressed, and were adapted to take a series of photos in quick succession as a plane flew over a target.

Camouflage

Britain and the United States adapted some of their fastest fighter planes for spying in World War II. The weapons were removed and the undersides were painted to blend in with the sky. Targets on the ground were disguised, too, and dummy vehicles and aircraft were created to fool enemy planes.

Height and endurance

In 1956, the United States unveiled a new type of spy plane—the U-2. Instead of being fast and agile, it was designed to fly great distances at great heights of up to 70,000 ft (21,000 m), beyond the reach of most planes and weapons. However, this didn't stop the Soviet Union from shooting one down in 1960.

Supersonic

The RF-101 Voodoo, shown here, was the first supersonic (faster than the speed of sound) reconnaissance aircraft. One of its many spy missions was during the Cuban Missile Crisis of the 1960s, to confirm that the Soviets had dismantled the missile sites they'd built just off the coast of the United States in Cuba.

Built for speed

The United States' next major spy plane was the Lockeed SR-71 "Blackbird." Used between 1964 and 1998, its main defense was its incredible speed. As the fastest jet-powered plane ever built, with a top speed of 2,193 mph (3,529 km/h), it could accelerate away from enemy planes and even missiles.

Endurance at sea

While many spy planes have been replaced with safer, unpiloted craft, one area in which spy planes are still used is maritime reconnaissance, scouring the seas for enemy submarines. Maritime spy planes like this British Hawker-Siddeley Nimrod are large and slow-moving to endure long flights.

Stealth

"Stealth" aircraft such as this B-2 Spirit bomber are unusual shapes and made of special materials that reduce their visibility, particularly to radar. Most are fighters and bombers, but a super-fast, super-secret stealth spy plane was rumored to have been made by the United States in the 1980s, codenamed "Aurora."

MQ-9 Reaper

Modern drones, such as this American-built MQ-9 Reaper, are equipped with both reconnaissance equipment for spying on the enemy, and missiles for taking them out. The Reaper can stay airborne for hours and has been used by the United States to patrol its borders, spying on people trying to enter the country illegally.

MAVs

Many experts believe that the future of UAVs will be miniature. Intelligence agencies are looking into creating tiny UAVs the size and shape of insects. Known as MAVs (micro aerial vehicles), they would have flapping wings, allowing them to hover unnoticed near a target while taking photos with a miniature camera.

Takeoff and touchdown

The Lightning Bug had to be launched from the underside of the wings of a much larger plane. The Bug didn't have landing gear (wheels), so once its mission was over, it would open a parachute to slow its fall, and would then be caught in midair by a helicopter.

Spy UAVs

After the Soviet Union shot down an American U-2 manned spy plane in 1960, the United States launched a program to create a spy UAV. The result was the jet-powered, camera-equipped Ryan 147 Lightning Bug, which flew on thousands of missions during the Vietnam War between 1964 and 1975.

Nuclear spies

In the 1950s, the United States converted several large B-17 bombers into UAVs. These planes were used for missions that were far too dangerous for manned aircraft, flying into the great mushroom clouds produced by nuclear bomb tests to collect data on the debris and radioactivity caused by the explosions.

Flying torpedoes

Unmanned radio-controlled planes were first developed in World War I. They weren't used for spying, however, but combat. Loaded with explosives and sent hurtling toward the enemy, these biplanes were flying torpedoes, capable of hitting targets 75 miles (120 km) away.

SPYING WITHOUT SPIES

Some aerial spying missions are just too dangerous for people. I should know—in World War I, the Germans equipped me with a tiny camera and sent me flying over the battlefields to photograph the enemy. UAVs (unmanned aerial vehicles) do an even better job than me—tackling hazardous missions to prevent real spies having to risk their necks.

Target drones

By the 1930s, several countries had produced radio-controlled aircraft, known as "drones," to act as targets for trainee gunners. The United States produced thousands of propeller-driven OQ-2 drones during World War II, and later developed fast-moving jet-powered UAVs, such as this Katydid drone.

V-1s and V-2s

The Germans had the deadliest UAVs in World War II. The V-1 (above) was a jet-powered flying bomb capable of traveling 155 miles (250 km) at 400 mph (640 km/h). This was followed by an even more fearsome weapon, the V-2 rocket (right), which could fly 200 miles (320 km) at a staggering 1,800 mph (2,880 km/h) and was the first man-made object to travel into space.

SECRET WEAPONS

A good spy needs to blend in with the crowd, not stand out.
But from time to time they may have to fight off an attacker,
or perhaps even "take out" an enemy target, particularly during
wartime. So it is essential to have a good weapons cabinet,
stocked with easily hidden, but deadly (and silent), devices.

SMALL WEAPONS

Spies like to use small, lightweight
weapons that are easy to carry and
easy to conceal (not to mention easy to
get rid off), such as daggers and pistols.

① Sten gun
Sometimes spies use larger weapons, but with
a few special spy adaptations. Many Allied spies
behind enemy lines in World War II had Sten
guns—a type of submachine gun that could be
broken into three small pieces for hiding.

HIDDEN WEAPONS

Even the smallest pistol or dagger
will be found if a spy is searched,
so they often disguise their weapons
as seemingly harmless objects.

② Bad news
KGB assassin Bogdan Stashinsky killed his targets
using a cyanide-gas-firing gun hidden in a rolled-up
newspaper. The gas gave the victims a heart attack,
so it looked like they died of natural causes.

③ Lipstick pistol
In the 1960s, the KGB developed a small gun
that was disguised as a woman's lipstick tube.
Known as the "kiss of death," it could fire just
a single shot—so the kiss had to be accurate.

④ Sleeve gun
Developed by the SOE in World War II,
the single-shot sleeve gun looked like
a simple metal tube and was hidden up
the spy's sleeve. To fire, the spy would
slide the gun into his hand and press
the trigger with his thumb.

⑤ Cell phone gun
This recent addition to a spy's arsenal
looks like a real cell phone, but the case
slides apart to reveal a four-shot
gun—press "5" to fire a round, but
beware: The shortness of the gun
makes it difficult to shoot accurately.

SILENT WEAPONS

Real spies need to do their jobs as silently and as secretly as possible, so they often choose quiet weapons such as crossbows and guns fitted with silencers.

⑥ Welrod

The SOE produced an extremely quiet gun known as the Welrod. It was designed to be used at very close range—ideally pressed right against the victim to further muffle the sound.

HIDDEN KNIVES

The secret knife has long been one of the most important tools in a spy's survival kit. They can be hidden up sleeves and behind lapels, and even disguised as credit cards.

⑦ Shoe knives

In World War II, Britain's SOE provided spies with deadly pairs of shoes. Some had curved knives that folded into the heels, while others had soles equipped with long, straight knives.

⑧ Coin knives

Consisting of a small, curved blade attached to the back of a coin by a hinge, coin knives were easily hidden in a pocketful of change, and were mainly used for acts of sabotage, such as cutting cables.

SNEAKY WEAPONS

Sneakiness is a quality all good spies need. They also need sneaky weapons to give them that extra edge.

⑨ Corner shot

This gun is the perfect sneaky spy rifle. Developed by Israel in the early 2000s, it pivots in the middle, allowing the spy to point it around corners. It has a front-mounted camera to show the target.

UNUSUAL EXPLOSIONS

Blowing things up is always easier if the enemy can't spot your bombs. Spies have used explosives disguised as all kinds of things.

⑩ Exploding coal

In World War II, Allied spies hid bombs in pieces of fake coal, which were painted to make sure they matched the real stuff before being planted in an enemy's fuel store and timed to explode.

⑪ Exploding rat

In a twist on the exploding coal idea, the SOE also booby-trapped a dead rat with explosives. The idea was to place it on a pile of coal so it would be shoveled onto the fire and, then, kaboom!

SHADY HISTORY

Spying is one of the world's oldest professions. Take a walk through the ages to discover the secret spying techniques of our ancestors, and meet some of the men and women (and animals) who have risked it all to join an illustrious group of super snoopers who have played a major part in shaping our history, from the ninja masters of stealth and disguise to the real James Bond.

SUN TZU

The year is 300 BCE and China is torn apart by endless warfare. I, Sun Tzu, military general, have learned through bitter struggle a mastery of tactics. To those who engage in battle, I offer this one idea: All warfare is based on deception, and from that single, simple truth you will find that the path to victory lies... in spies!

Make use of spies

Rather than confronting a powerful enemy head-on, it is better to learn his plans in advance using spies. Good information makes wars quicker, saving you money and men. But the world is filled with devious people, and only a wise ruler can learn the difference between a good adviser and a treacherous spy.

A spy for every job

In spying, as in everything, there are many ways to skin a cat:

Doomed spies can be told a lie and sent into the enemy camp to spread the false news. No matter if they are caught and killed.

A poor enemy can usually be bribed to betray a rich master.

Make use of anger or greed: A court official with a grudge, a jealous lover, or a greedy courtier can all become valuable "inside spies."

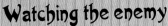

Brave survivor spies are willing to risk all to bring back news from behind enemy lines.

When an assassin kills an enemy lord, the lord's followers will soon run away. As the saying goes, when the tree falls, the monkeys scatter.

Best of all are turned spies, double agents who can control others around them.

Watching the enemy

A good spy watches the world like a hawk. They are ruthless in their actions, like a wolf.

When chariots approach, dust spurts high and straight. But if the dust wanders far and wide, foot soldiers are on their way.

If officers get angry, it's a sign that their men are tired or restless.

When birds gather above campsites, those campsites are empty.

If you see soldiers leaning on their spears, attack soon for they are weak for want of food.

A final word: Although you have no wings, learn to fly. A speedy escape will save your skin if you are in danger.

CHANAKYA

IT IS 300 BCE AND MY LORD AND MASTER KING CHANDRAGUPTA RULES OVER A MIGHTY ASIAN EMPIRE STRETCHING ACROSS INDIA, PAKISTAN, AND AFGHANISTAN. I, CHANAKYA, HIS LOYAL SERVANT, AM NEVER FAR FROM HIS SIDE— AS ADVISER, GENERAL, AND SPYMASTER. ALLOW ME TO SHARE MY KNOWLEDGE OF THE SECRET ARTS.

Spy tactics

Be on your guard, for enemy spies are always at work. To protect my lord against them, first I learn how to think as they do. I study my enemy's lands and watch them closely to discover their habits and their appearance, even when they are in disguise. And I always sleep alone, since who knows what words I babble when I am asleep? Above all else, I make sure my information is correct before taking action, or I will be no better than a diver leaping into a pool after the tide has gone out.

Know your enemy

Permanent spies stay close to the king, his ministers, and generals. Beware: Some are disguised as fortune-tellers or holy men so that people will tell them their secrets.

Wandering spies move about the country. Some are trained in science and the sorcerer's arts. Others, who are naturally cruel, concoct potions to strike down their enemies.

Beware the fortune-teller!

Learn their methods

I have come across many fiendish and dirty tricks in my time. Be on the lookout for foreign spies who will burn your stores and crops.

Sssssss!

Sneaky spies drive snakes mad by smearing the blood of muskrats in their eyes— then release them among your soldiers.

Savage spies dressed as demons may parade up and down outside your walls, filling the air with the horrific cries of jackals and antelopes. Pay no attention, for they wish to strike fear into your heart. Beneath their robes, they are but ordinary men.

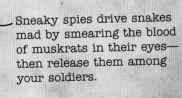

If a stranger hands me a drink, I take care, for it may be laced with the poisonous juice of the madana plant.

Such warnings I give, so that you may not wallow in folly and ignorance.

STARRING HASSAN-I-SABBAH AS THE GRAND HEADMASTER IN

MISSION: ASSASSIN

It's the 11th century. A war over the Holy Land rages in the Middle East, between the Christian crusaders from Europe and rival Muslim sects. Charismatic Hassan-i-Sabbah, an Ismaili Muslim missionary, has a new way of waging war: His small but fearsome group, trained in espionage tactics, exerts its power by ruthlessly murdering those who oppose it. The fame of the Assassins spreads—by the 13th century, when the word *assassin* is whispered in Europe, a professional murderer is about to strike.

STARRING:
The Grand Priors as Hassan's trusted commanders
The Propagandists as his recruiters and masters of persuasion
The Rafiqs as the initiated graduates of agent training
The Lasiqs as the unquestioningly loyal self-sacrificing agents

122

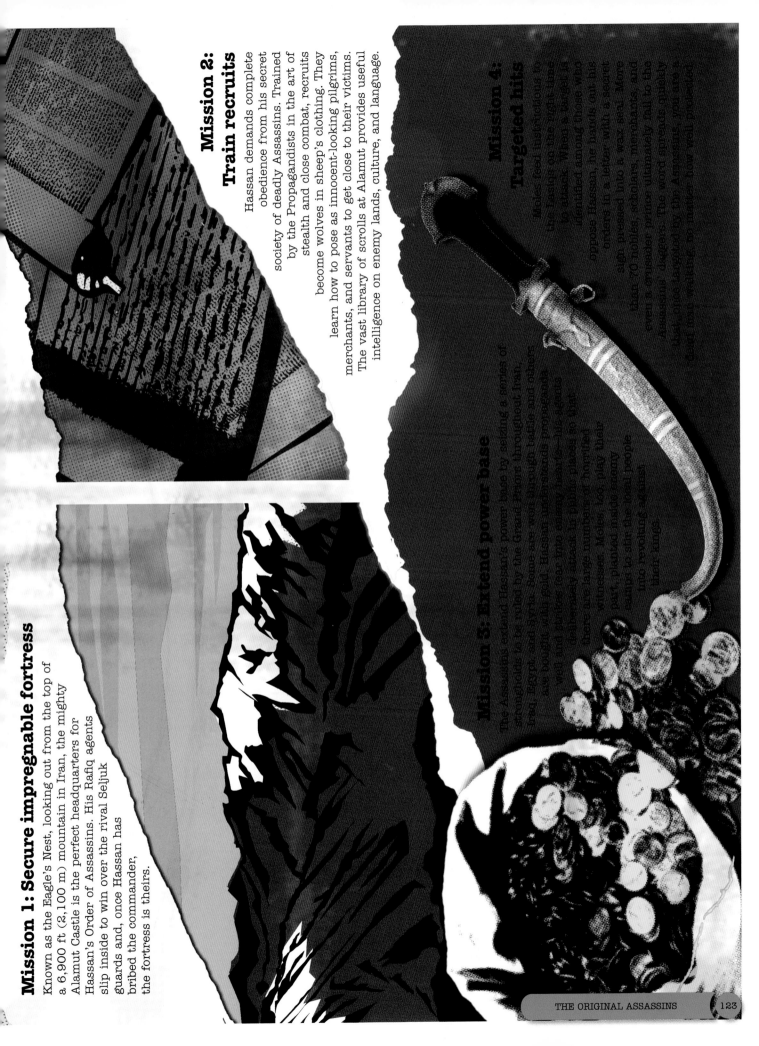

Mission 1: Secure impregnable fortress

Known as the Eagle's Nest, looking out from the top of a 6,900 ft (2,100 m) mountain in Iran, the mighty Alamut Castle is the perfect headquarters for Hassan's Order of Assassins. His Rafiq agents slip inside to win over the rival Seljuk guards and, once Hassan has bribed the commander, the fortress is theirs.

Mission 2: Train recruits

Hassan demands complete obedience from his secret society of deadly Assassins. Trained by the Propagandists in the art of stealth and close combat, recruits become wolves in sheep's clothing. They learn how to pose as innocent-looking pilgrims, merchants, and servants to get close to their victims. The vast library of scrolls at Alamut provides useful intelligence on enemy lands, culture, and language.

Mission 3: Extend power base

The Assassins extend Hassan's power base by seizing a series of strongholds to be ruled by the Grand Priors throughout Iran, Iraq, Egypt, and Syria. Some are won through battle and others are bought with gold. Hassan sends his envoys as propaganda well and bribes fee) into enemy land—his agents deliberately attack in public places so that there are large numbers of horrified witnesses. Mobs Vicki play their part, planted inside many camps to stir the local people into revolting against their kings.

Mission 4: Targeted hits

Hassan feed instructions to the Fedayin on the right time to attack. When a target is identified among those who oppose Hassan, he hands out his orders in a letter with a secret sign pressed into a wax seal. More than 70 nobles, scholars, merchants, and even a caliphon prince ultimately fall to the Assassins' daggers. The word spreads quickly that once targeted by the Assassins, you are a dead man walking, no matter how well protected.

① THIRD TIME'S THE CHARM

The Roman Emperor Nero (37–68 CE) decided to kill his mother Agrippina by turning her bed into a crushing contraption. It worked—on a poor slave sent to warm the bed. Plan B: a ship that sank itself. Although it sank, Agrippina made it to shore. In the end, one of his agents stabbed her to death. Simple!

② THE SPY WHO BLEW IT

A group of Catholics planned to blow up English King James I on November 5, 1605, and placed 36 barrels of gunpowder under the House of Lords. But the king caught wind of the plot after one of the conspirators warned a friend to stay away. D'oh!

RETURNED PACKAGES

③ POISON PEAS

In 1776, during the American Revolution, a treacherous guard supposedly tried to poison George Washington's favorite dish—green peas. But Washington, warned by his housekeeper, threw them out of the window and watched as hens pecked at the peas and clucked their last.

④ OPERATION OVERKILL

Giuseppe Marco Fieschi invented a mega-gun with 20 barrels in order to kill King Louis Philippe of France. In July 1835, he blasted away with his "infernal machine." When the smoke cleared, 3 horses and 18 people were dead, but his bullets had only grazed the king's head.

⑤ MISSED BY A NOSE

On April 7, 1926, Violet Gibson, a 50-year-old Irish aristocrat, tried to assassinate Benito Mussolini, the fascist leader of Italy. She shot him three times at close range—as he proudly raised his head to listen to the fascist anthem—but the bullets merely nicked his nostrils.

⑥ DEATH BY CHOCOLATE

In 1956, MI6 deputy head George Young hatched many bungled plans to kill Egyptian president Gamal Nasser—from canisters of nerve gas to cigarette packs firing poison darts. His idea of sweet revenge was a box of chocolates injected with a lethal poison. Like the others, it failed to bite.

⑦ SHELL SHOCK

In the 1960s, the CIA tried but failed to harm Fidel Castro, Communist leader of Cuba. They planted radioactive chemicals in his shoes to make his famous beard fall out, poisoned his cigars with botulism bacteria, and even created an exploding conch shell to blow up the scuba-loving premier!

⑧ LINKS TO THE ENEMY

In 1964, Trayco Belopopsky, a Bulgarian defector studying at Cambridge University, received a surprise visit from his father, who brought him some Bulgarian sausages. But when he tossed one to a stray dog, it died horribly. The sausages had been spiked by Service 7, the Bulgarian intelligence agency's hit squad.

⑨ THE UNSOLVED SOUP

During a bitter election in 2004, Ukraine's opposition leader Viktor Yushchenko became sick after eating a bowl of soup. Doctors found huge levels of the poison dioxin in his bloodstream. Yushchenko pointed the finger at government agents, but the real story remains to be told.

TARGET STILL STANDING

It seemed like a good idea at the time, then it all went horribly wrong. Some assassination plots go off the rails; others are just plain crazy. When assassinations fail, do bad assassins blame their tools?

INVISIBLE SPIES

Bold ninja, the enemy lord lies sleeping in yonder castle. Creep in like the spider. Keep a keen ear and a sharp eye, then strike hard and fast like the cobra. Your work done, vanish like mist on the wind. Although you must conquer heaven and earth to complete your mission, remember that you are born into the house of the shadow warriors. And if the end comes... die well!

ACROSS THE MOAT

No need for disguise. A wise agent knows the darkness is his ally, and robes of darkest blue will hide you in the shadows. To keep your explosives dry, trust your hooked rope to take you high above the moat, then scale the walls with your claws of iron.

A WAY IN

Climb high to where the stone walls turn to wood. Your fingertips will tell you where the stockade is weak. A loose board can be pried open with a metal bar, while the razor-sharp teeth of your folding saw, or *hamagari*, can cut a way in.

TASTE OF DEATH

Your *inro*—or medicine carrier—is packed with deadly potions and poisons. Find a gap in the ceiling big enough to lower a fine cord of silk through. Use it to trickle a few drops of poison into the mouths of the sleeping guards. Sweet dreams!

MASTER OF CHAOS

Let the mayhem begin! Hurl explosives wrapped in a jacket of iron and pottery to cut the enemy to shreds. Then fling paper parcels packed with poison to fill the fortress with fatal fumes. The guards will fall and splutter as you dash stealthily toward your ultimate target.

SILENT STEPS

Forget not the words of the ancient sages: "Silence is a friend who will never betray!" Walk with feet of velvet for there are traps everywhere. Enemy guards lurk behind sliding doors, while "nightingale floors" chirp loudly, no matter how gently you tread on them.

LISTEN UP

Yes, a ninja brings death and destruction, but you are here to learn the battle plans of your enemies. Now is the time to use your *saoto hikigane*— a device shaped like an ear trumpet. Listen in on your enemies' whispers and note the movements of the guards.

STAR WARS

Take caution... more guards appear, having heard the death cries of their own! Draw your bow and set the wooden walls ablaze with flaming arrows. While confusion reigns, dispatch as many guards as you can. Throwing stars will strike them down from a distance.

THE FINAL BLOW

The night should not end well for the lord of the castle. A single slash from your sword and the deed is done. But danger there always is. The heavy club he keeps has already crushed the skulls of two would-be assassins.

SAYONARA SAMURAI

Make good your escape. Use your hooked rope to rappel down the castle walls. Then pick up the wooden water shoes hidden in the bushes to cross the nearby swamp. Once across, vanish into the undergrowth. Truly can one soldier become an army!

THE TEENAGE NINJA

IT'S THE YEAR 1333. FOR 150 YEARS, JAPAN HAS BEEN RULED BY THE SHOGUNS, WARLORDS BACKED BY THE SAMURAI—A CLASS OF HIGHLY SKILLED WARRIORS. WHEN EMPEROR GO-DAIGO TRIES TO WIN BACK POWER, HELPED BY REBELS LOYAL TO THE THRONE, JAPAN IS PLUNGED INTO CIVIL WAR.

WITHIN THREE YEARS, THE REBELS ARE BEATEN. GENERAL ASHIKAGA TAKAUJI BECOMES THE NEW SHOGUN. THE EMPEROR IS BANISHED, ALONG WITH HIS SUPPORTERS. ONE OF THE REBEL LORDS, SUKETOMO, IS SENT TO THE ISLAND OF SADO. HERE, THE WARRIOR MONK HOMMA SABURO HAS BEEN GIVEN ORDERS TO EXECUTE HIM.

THE SON OF LORD SUKETOMO, KUMAWAKA, TRAVELS MANY MILES TO SEE HIS FATHER ONE LAST TIME, BUT SABURO CRUELLY KILLS HIS FATHER BEFORE KUMAWAKA HAS A CHANCE TO SAY GOODBYE. HE SWEARS REVENGE.

I MAY BE NO MATCH FOR YOU IN BATTLE, SABURO, BUT I SWEAR I'LL KILL YOU!

KUMAWAKA FEIGNS ILLNESS, AND SABURO IS BOUND BY DUTY TO LOOK AFTER HIM UNTIL HE RECOVERS. WHILE EVERYONE SLEEPS, KUMAWAKA SPIES ON SABURO'S GUARDS AND LEARNS THEIR ROUTINES.

AHA! SO SABURO SLEEPS ALONE!

ONE STORMY NIGHT, KUMAWAKA DECIDES TO STRIKE. HE SLIPS PAST THE GUARDS IN THE POURING RAIN.

KUMAWAKA HAS NO WEAPONS, BUT LIKE ALL GOOD NINJA HE THINKS ON HIS FEET.

I'LL SNATCH SABURO'S SWORD AND KILL HIM WITH HIS OWN WEAPON.

SABURO ALWAYS SLEEPS WITH A LIT LAMP IN HIS ROOM. HOW CAN KUMAWAKA PULL SABURO'S SWORD FROM ITS SCABBARD BEFORE THE MONK AWAKES?

KUMAWAKA SEES MOTHS OUTSIDE THE ROOM ATTRACTED TO THE LIGHT INSIDE. HE PULLS THE SLIDING DOOR OPEN SLIGHTLY, SO THAT THE MOTHS FLUTTER IN AND GATHER AROUND THE LAMP, BLOCKING ITS LIGHT.

NOW THE DARKNESS WILL HIDE ME. REVENGE WILL BE MINE!

NGGGHHH!

KUMAWAKA FLEES, BUT HIS BLOODY FOOTPRINTS SOON GIVE HIM AWAY. WITH THE GUARDS HOT ON HIS TRAIL, HE FINDS THE PATH BLOCKED BY A DEEP MOAT THAT SURROUNDS THE CASTLE.

I'LL NEVER JUMP ACROSS!

THINKING QUICKLY, KUMAWAKA NIMBLY CLIMBS ONTO A BAMBOO PLANT. IT BENDS UNDER HIS WEIGHT, FORMING A NATURAL BRIDGE ACROSS THE RIVER.

KUMAWAKA VANISHES INTO THE NIGHT. ALTHOUGH A HUNDRED MEN HUNT FOR HIM, HE ESCAPES AND CATCHES A BOAT TO THE MAINLAND—AND SAFETY.

KUMAWAKA'S STORY APPEARS IN THE EPIC HISTORY *THE TAIHEIKI* AND IS THE FIRST KNOWN NINJA-STYLE ASSASSINATION. INSPIRED BY KUMAWAKA'S DEADLY TACTICS, WITHIN 100 YEARS THE NINJA—MEANING "THE PEOPLE WHO STEAL AWAY"—WERE FEARED ACROSS JAPAN AS HIRED SPIES, SABOTEURS AND ASSASSINS.

THE PILLOW SNATCHER

MOST SAMURAI FOLLOWED STRICT RULES OF HONOR AND COMBAT. BUT STARTING IN THE MID-15TH CENTURY, A FEW SAMURAI CLANS (THE NINJA) DEVELOPED THE SHADOWY ARTS OF SPYING, UNDERCOVER WARFARE, AND ASSASSINATION. THESE SKILLS WERE PASSED DOWN FROM FATHER TO SON.

AAAARRRGGH!

NOT NOW, SON, I'VE HAD A LONG DAY.

BY THE MID-17TH CENTURY, THIS TRADITION HAD DIED OUT. JAPAN'S WARLORDS NOW RELIED ON NINJA SCHOOLS TO TRAIN SPIES AND ASSASSINS. ONE SCHOOL WAS RUN BY NAKAGAWA SHOSHUNJIN, AN EXPERT NINJA. IT WAS SAID HE HAD MAGICAL POWERS AND COULD TURN HIMSELF INTO A SNAKE, RAT, OR BAT.

IN REALITY, SHOSHUNJIN WAS NO SORCERER, BUT A MASTER OF STEALTH.

ONE DAY, SHOSHUNJIN WAS ASKED TO VISIT THE TSUGARU CLAN'S CASTLE. THE FAMILY NEEDED NINJA IN ITS ARMY, AND TSUGARU GEMBAN, HEARING THE RUMORS OF SHOSHUNJIN'S POWERS, WANTED TO PUT HIS SKILLS TO THE TEST.

IF YOU'RE SO SNEAKY, TRY STEALING MY PILLOW AS I SLEEP.

JUST SAY WHEN, MY LORD!

THAT NIGHT, AS GEMBAN LAY DOWN ON HIS FUTON, HE HEARD THE PITTER-PATTER OF RAIN OUTSIDE IN THE COURTYARD.

I CERTAINLY WON'T GET ANY SLEEP WITH ALL THAT THUNDER.

GEMBAN STAYED PUT WITH HIS HEAD ON THE PILLOW—HE DIDN'T WANT TO MAKE IT EASY FOR SHOSHUNJIN. BUT THEN A FEW DROPS OF WATER SPLASHED ON HIS FACE.

THE ROOF IS LEAKING!

TO GET A BETTER LOOK, GEMBAN RAISED HIS HEAD OFF THE PILLOW FOR AN INSTANT...

WHAAAAT?!

STANDING BESIDE GEMBAN—AS HE RUBBED HIS SORE HEAD—WAS SHOSHUNJIN, GRINNING FROM EAR TO EAR.

SORRY, BUT IT WAS YOUR IDEA.

GEMBAN KNEW THAT HERE WAS A NINJA OF GREAT SKILL, AND ALSO SOMEONE TO BE TRUSTED.

YOU'RE HIRED!

SHOSHUNJIN PICKED A GROUP OF 20 YOUNG SAMURAI TO TRAIN AS NINJA FOR THE TSUGARU CLAN. HE NAMED THEM *HAYAMICHI NO MONO*, THE "SHORTCUT PEOPLE."

WATCH OUT, I'VE GOT A BLACK BELT IN ORIGAMI!

THE NINJA TRAINED IN COMPLETE SECRECY IN THE SOUTHEAST CORNER OF THE TSUGARU CASTLE. IN FACT, ONLY GEMBAN AND THE HEAD OF THE TSUGARU CLAN EVEN KNEW THESE SHADOW WARRIORS EXISTED!

AAAARRGGH!

OUCH!

AAIIIIEEE!

HEY, DO YOU HEAR THAT? WHAT IS IT?

NO IDEA, BUT I'M GLAD I'M OUT HERE!

THE POISONER'S HANDBOOK

A spy receives orders to assassinate an enemy of the state. Sure, shooting or blowing up the victim will send out a stark warning, but if discretion is required, poison is the ultimate stealth killer. A tiny dose will complete the job and can be almost impossible to detect. Some poisons can kill a victim in just seconds, while others may take days or even weeks to take effect—plenty of time for the culprit to flee the scene!

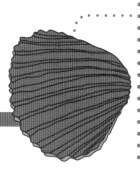

SEAFOOD SUICIDE

During the Cold War, spies carried well-hidden suicide pills. In case of capture, the American U-2 spy pilot Gary Powers carried his, rather imaginatively, in a hollow silver dollar. If swallowed, the saxitoxins (poison from shellfish) inside the pill could kill within 10 seconds, giving the enemy no chance of retrieving secrets from him.

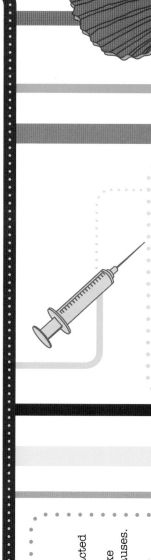

SILENT BUT DEADLY

In 1938, the sweet-smelling liquid chloroform was used to knock out Abram Slutsky, head of the Soviet foreign intelligence. He was then injected in the arm with a fatal poison, hydrocyanic acid, which made it look like he had a heart attack. He was one of hundreds of thousands of victims executed during the Great Purge in the Soviet Union, ordered by Joseph Stalin.

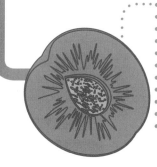

JUST PEACHY!

Cyanide was first discovered by the ancient Egyptians who extracted it from peach pits. It induces a heart attack, making it look like the victim has died of natural causes. In 1959, this heart-stopper was the favorite poison of KGB agent Bogdan Stashinsky who murdered the Ukrainian politician Stepan Bandera, with cyanide gas.

ASSASSIN'S DIARY

In the 1500s, arsenic was the poison of choice for assassins hired by Venice's secretive Council of Ten. The council's cloak-and-dagger poison antics were recorded in a thin book marked *Secreto Secretissima* ("Top Top Secret"). Colorless and odorless, arsenic causes vomiting, blindness, and often death.

WICKED WALLETS

In the 1920s, the Soviet intelligence agency, known then as the Cheka, set up a factory called the Kamera, to invent poisons and assassination tools. The Cheka's successor, the KGB—formed in 1954—developed a poison-releasing wallet. When the trigger was pulled, a glass capsule containing the poison was crushed inside, releasing a deadly gas.

A LETHAL HANDSHAKE

During the 1950s, as the Cold War against the United States gathered momentum, the Kamera (which was now part of the KGB) continued to invent a range of small but menacing tools of the trade. These included a ring with a turquoise stone that, when unscrewed, revealed a sharp point covered with a deadly poison.

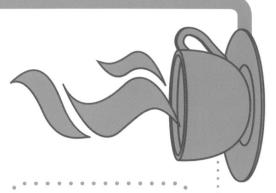

DEADLY DRINK

The KGB Kamera also developed a plutonium dust that, when inhaled, gave the victim a fatal cancer. Years later, in 2006, former Russian agent Alexander Litvinenko died after drinking tea laced with polonium-210—another deadly radioactive element. His killer has yet to be brought to justice.

THE MEAN BEAN

Ricin is found in the bean of the castor plant, and can easily be hidden in food and drink... or even an umbrella! In 1978, a ricin pellet was fired from a modified umbrella, into the leg of Georgi Markov, a Bulgarian dissident. Within just four days, he had died from heart failure.

HORSE DROPS

During World War I, German agent Karl Boy-Ed arranged for animals, including horses, to be infected with glanders—an infectious and deadly disease—and then sent to France and Britain. This was very bad news for soldiers there, since they were heavily dependent on horses for transporting artillery and supply convoys.

NEEDLING THE ENEMY

During World War II, Major Christopher Clayton Hutton of MI9 (part of the British military intelligence) developed an air gun for the French Resistance. It looked like a pen and fired phonograph needles. The French spread a rumor that the needles were coated in a deadly poison—they weren't, but the threat was enough to deter the Germans.

DEATH IN THE SHADOWS

Coming to a head in the 16th century, there was an explosion of spy activity all around the world. Ruthless rulers from Peru to China used spies to round up rebels and conquer new lands, while the battle between Catholics and Protestants in Europe led to new "saintly" spies. With armies of agents lurking in the shadows, these were dark days.

THE MERCILESS MING

You wouldn't mess with the merciless Ming Dynasty in China. In the late 1360s, Emperor Hongwu set up the dreaded Jinyi Wei or "Embroidered Uniform Guard"—a spy network with 14,000 agents. Created to root out rebels, its agents were often corrupt. Anyone refusing to pay a bribe got flung in prison and tortured to death, and by the 16th century, the Jinyi Wei was silencing Ming opponents left and right.

THE HEADHUNTER

Elizabeth I's spymaster, Sir Francis Walsingham, uncovered several plots to overthrow the Protestant queen and replace her with her cousin, Mary, Queen of Scots, but he couldn't pin anything on Mary herself. Mary sent coded messages to her Catholic supporters in France and Spain, smuggled in beer barrels and hidden in the heels of the shoes worn by her fashionable couriers. Unfortunately for Mary, Walsingham knew about the messages, and after decoding them, he had the evidence he needed: On February 8, 1587, off came her head!

OVERRUN

In the 15th century, the Incas were looking to extend their empire by conquering other tribes. The *sapa* (chief) sent spies to snoop on the enemy and intelligence would be reported back by quick-footed couriers, or *chasqui*, who ran relays to cover 150 miles (240 km) in a day. When victory was secured, the enemy chiefs would be told that they could keep their tribal chiefdoms if they surrendered to the Inca empire.

THE TERRIFIED TSAR

The paranoid Russian tsar Ivan IV (1530–1584), nicknamed "the Terrible," was convinced that assassins lurked around every corner. To destroy them, he set up Russia's first spy network—the Oprichnina. Dressed in black, its 6,000 agents rode horses with saddles that bore a dog's head and broom—symbols that their mission was to sniff out treason and sweep it away.

THE BLACK CHAMBER

Nicknamed the "Red Eminence" due to his scarlet clerical robes, Cardinal Richelieu was the most powerful man in France for much of the 17th century. To keep an eye on rebellious nobles and Protestant rebels, he formed a secret police squad known as the "Black Chamber," which was at the heart of a spy web operating across Europe. Many of his agents were priests and monks—for who would suspect a man of god?

CHAMBER OF HORRORS

Priest-hunter Richard Topcliffe was notoriously happy to help Sir Francis Walsingham torture enemy spies until they cracked. Topcliffe dreamed up a hideous rack that stretched victims' bodies until their limbs were torn apart, or used spiked rollers to rip victims to shreds (below). Other much-loved torture tools included the bone-crunching Scavenger's Daughter, or the Pit—a deep well filled with rats and filthy water.

HOLY SPIES

In the 1580s, Spain and France sent Jesuit priests to Protestant England to support Catholics living there, and to spy on English forces. Their foreign accents and clothing often gave them away, so these holy spies took refuge in secret "priest holes" built under trapdoors.

THE V TEAM

In 1582, a treaty between France and Spain threatened the Italian city of Venice. The Venetians immediately dispatched 30 spies to discover what that threat was, but the treaty was sealed inside a metal tube chained to a courier's wrist. After drugging the courier, the team removed and copied the treaty before sealing it back inside so that no one was any the wiser... except for the Venetians, of course.

CAUGHT!

Spying is a risky business, and the chance of getting caught grows with every move a spy makes. It can take years to get ahold of useful top-secret information, but a spy's career can be over in the blink of an eye if he or she is caught in the act. Unless there's a spy swap in the offing, a captured spy can face a long spell in prison... or a speedy execution.

No way back

During the American Revolution (1775–1783), British Major John André got ahold of drawings showing how the rebel fort of West Point, New York, could be taken. Riding back to British lines, he was stopped by an American patrol. He decided to bribe the guards. Bad move – André was found guilty of spying and swiftly hanged.

A tree-mendous spy

In the 1960s, Israeli agent Elie Cohen posed as a wealthy Arab businessman while spying on Syrian forces. Following Cohen's advice, the Syrians planted eucalyptus trees to hide their bunkers. But this actually identified them as targets for Israeli planes during the Arab-Israeli war of 1967. Cohen was caught while sending a radio message in 1965. He was tried and hanged before seeing the results of his mission.

Kept in the dark

In 1958, North Korean commando Woo Yong-gak was captured on a spying mission aboard a boat off the coast of South Korea. He was released in 1999, 41 years later. He had spent most of that time on his own in a cold, dark cell just 10 ft (5 m) wide. His first words on his release were: "I'm happy to see light."

I don't feel well... honest!

In the Civil War (1861–1865), Union spy Pauline Cushman stole battle plans from Confederate officers but was caught. Sentenced to death, the former actress feigned illness to delay the execution, but then made a miraculous recovery when invading Union troops forced her captors to retreat.

A brave farewell

No general could resist the charms of Dutch dancer Mata Hari (real name Margaretha Zelle), so when World War I broke out, a German agent thought she would make the perfect spy! She didn't. Poor Hari was soon outed by French agents. The penalty: death. Refusing a blindfold, she bravely blew a kiss to the firing squad.

Hello, dolly

During World War II, American Velvalee Dickinson used her doll shop as a cover to send intelligence to Japanese agents in South America. Her notes contained coded messages about U.S. Navy defenses. She was finally caught when one of her contacts moved and her messages were returned. Her sentence: 10 years in jail and a $10,000 fine.

Suicide pill

In the 1970s, during the Cold War between the United States and the Soviet Union, Soviet diplomat Aleksandr Ogorodnik copied secret documents for the CIA using a miniature spy camera. Code-named Trigon, he was eventually exposed by a KGB mole inside the CIA. He swallowed a poison suicide pill shortly after his arrest.

A traitor's death

Oleg Penkovsky was a Soviet double agent who passed the CIA the plans of missile sites in fellow Communist country Cuba during the Cuban Missile Crisis. But in October 1962, he was betrayed by a KGB mole within the CIA and arrested. Some say he was shot in the head after a short trial, while others claim he was burned alive as a warning to other traitors.

ESCAPE ARTISTS

Most spies expect to get caught at some point, but the secret to survival is to give nothing away while hatching a cunning escape plan. From hiding tools in plates of food to dressing as a woman, captured spies have pulled off some jaw-dropping jailbreaks.

❶ A JUICY ESCAPE

Catholic priest John Gerard was a spy in Protestant England, with espionage orders direct from the pope himself. A master of disguise, Gerard hid from the English authorities for eight years before being arrested by Queen Elizabeth I's soldiers and thrown into the Tower of London in 1594. He immediately began plotting his escape, contacting his comrades by smuggling out notes written in invisible ink made from orange juice. The notes directed his accomplices to row a boat into the Tower's moat and swing a rope up to his cell. Gerard almost fell to his death while climbing down the rope, but managed to escape. He was smuggled out of England as one of the very few escapees from the Tower of London.

❷ ROMANTIC GETAWAY

Part-time spy and full-time ladies' man Giacomo Casanova was locked up on the seventh floor of the doge's (duke's) palace in Venice for a series of crimes, including offenses against the Church. He smuggled a metal bar into his cell, sharpened it into a spike, and then tricked a guard into taking the bar to a priest in a nearby cell by hiding it in a Bible under a plate of pasta. The priest used the bar to first make a hole in his ceiling, and then in Casanova's. The two men used the trusty bar again to help them break through the lead roof at the top of the prison. Using ropes and ladders, they scaled down the seven floors to the ground and escaped by gondola into the city's network of canals.

❸ DEAD MAN RUNNING

Edward Yeo-Thomas was no stranger to danger: During the Russian Civil War (1917–1923), he escaped from a Communist prison in Poland after strangling a guard. During World War II, using the code name "The White Rabbit," he worked as a British secret agent in France, but was arrested and tortured by the Gestapo (the German secret police). He was sent to Buchenwald concentration camp but a sympathetic guard helped transfer him to a camp for French prisoners of war by swapping identities with a French prisoner who had died of typhus. This made escape easier, but it took a few failed attempts before he finally reached the Allied troops, and freedom, in April 1945.

❹ OVERDRESSED

In 1941, the Nazi German spy Günter Schütz was caught within hours of parachuting into Ireland on his first spying mission. He made friends with Jim Van Loon, a Dutch Nazi, while imprisoned in Dublin's Mountjoy Prison. Together they planned their escape. First, they tried to dig their way out, but their tunnel filled with water. Undeterred, the duo patiently sawed through the iron bars of their cell's window and successfully escaped down a makeshift rope ladder. Using clothes smuggled in, Schütz disguised himself as a woman before scaling the 18 ft (5 m) high prison wall. He spent two months on the run but was recaptured and imprisoned for the rest of the war.

❺ GIVING THE SLIP

Opera singer Margery Booth spied on Nazi Germany for Britain before and during World War II. Her popularity with Adolf Hitler and his henchmen put her above suspicion, enabling her to work with British spy John Brown, gathering information on British traitors working with the Nazis. On one occasion, Brown hastily shoved secret papers down her dress moments before she was about to perform at Berlin's opera house. Eventually, the Nazis became suspicious and she was arrested and tortured by the Gestapo. Admitting nothing, she was released and later made her escape from Berlin during an air raid. After returning to Britain, however, she found it difficult to find work, since people thought she was a traitor.

❻ A SPY YARN

In 1961, British secret service officer George Blake was sentenced to 42 years in a London prison for being a KGB spy, after he had betrayed dozens of British agents working in the Middle East. Five years later, two of Blake's fellow prisoners, who had just been released, helped him escape. They fashioned a lightweight but sturdy ladder from knitting needles and rope and threw it up to Blake's window. Using the ladder to scale down the wall, he fell and broke his wrist, but still managed to make it to the getaway car. Blake was smuggled out of Britain and eventually made his way to Moscow where he received one of the Soviet Union's highest honors—the Order of Friendship—for his services to Soviet espionage.

A SPY'S BEST FRIEND

Welcome to Shady Acres, a retirement home for elderly animal agents. During World War II, more than 40 animals in Britain alone were awarded the Dickin Medal for bravery and, to this day, animals continue to be the secret weapons behind many operations, sniffing out enemy agents and risking life and limb to carry urgent messages. Brave, resourceful, and packed with super senses, we salute you!

TRUSTY STEED

Neigh there! For centuries, army scouts have ridden on horseback to spy on enemies or carry messages. In the 13th century, I rode with the Mongol leader Genghis Khan. His army covered great distances. Don't be fooled by the old geezer you see now: Back in the day, I could gallop at 31 mph (50 km/h) in short bursts, and travel more than 124 miles (200 km) in 24 hours!

BRAVE MESSENGER

Homing pigeons have been used since ancient times to carry messages, thanks to our ability to fly in darkness and storms at breakneck speeds. My great-grandfather, Cher Ami, flew through a hail of bullets in World War I to deliver a message that saved hundreds of American soldiers. Me, I was a bit of a looker once and trained in World War II to attract German spy pigeons carrying secrets out of Britain. I caused quite a flutter!

SPY CATCHER

Ruff! Sergeant Stubby reporting for duty. The most decorated dog of World War I, I took part in 17 battles. I'm best known for grabbing a German spy by the seat of his pants after hearing a noise in the dark. The spy tried to run for it, but I tripped him up and hung on until my handler, Corporal Robert Conroy, arrived.

MARINE MAULER

Forget Flipper! In the 1970s and 1980s, I was a lean, mean counterintelligence machine. As one of the dolphins trained by the U.S. Navy Marine Mammal Program, I protected ships and ports against enemy agents or saboteurs in the water. My task was to spot enemy divers, sneak up behind them, then attach a device to their air tanks that made them float to the surface.

SUPER-SNIFFER

I'm the big fish around here! I have a large snout, sensitive nostrils, and a large part of my brain is dedicated to smell—all perfect for tracking enemy spies. A special implant in my brain allows scientists to steer me toward suspicious targets. In the future, sharks like me could become stealth spies, capable of following enemy vessels for days without being spotted.

CYBORG

We may be the new mechanical bugs on the block, but high stress has led to early retirement. When we were just nymphs back in the 1970s, scientists jammed electrodes and tiny video cameras into our bodies. As we developed, our bodies grew around these implants, encasing them within us. A handy bugging device, we buzzed around so that our high-tech insides, which were linked to the boss's computer, picked up images and sounds.

TRICKY OPERATORS

I'm Micky, and his name's Tricky. We were trained by MI6 at Porton Down, Britain's top secret military research center, to help bug the apartment of a suspected Russian spy in Lisbon.

Back in the early 1990s, we carried a wire down through the bends in a drainpipe to a receiver in an apartment below the suspect's home. Exciting times. Another mouse, Thicky, wasn't up to the job and was sent home in disgrace.

ACOUSTIC KITTY

Can you see the microphone sewn into my head and the antenna in my tail? Purrrfectly horrible! In the 1960s, the CIA operation "Acoustic Kitty" tried using cool cats like me to listen in on secret spy conversations, but I was far more interested in looking for food. Speaking of which, do I see small mice?

Huh?

THE THINKER

Good evening. My name is Maurice Oldfield, but you can call me Sir Maurice. I was head of Britain's MI6 from 1973 to 1978. I'm no match for Bond with my pudgy face and thick glasses, but when British actor Sir Alec Guinness played the Cold War spy and all-around clever chap George Smiley (based on John le Carré's thrilling novels), he copied his character—and his haircut—from me.

THE BOOKWORM

In the action film *Patriot Games*, Jack Ryan—played by Hollywood hero Harrison Ford—is a U.S. Navy lecturer and retired CIA analyst who returns to the CIA after foiling an attack on the British royal family. Ford based his performance on none other than yours truly, Professor Craig Symonds, shadowing me at the U.S. Naval Academy in Maryland.

THE DASHING RESCUER

Sacré bleu! It drives me mad to hear talk of Baroness Orczy's made-up tale of Sir Percy Blakeney and his alter ego spy, the Scarlet Pimpernel. I, Baron de Batz, am ze real deal. During the French Revolution, I raised secret funds for ze royal family, and in 1793 was this close to rescuing King Louis XVI before the guillotine chopped off his head!

BEHIND THE MASK

There's the murmur of polite conversation and the clink of glasses at this lavish masquerade ball. But take a good look around and you'll see that not everything is as it seems. For every James Bond or Scarlet Pimpernel, there's a real-life secret agent behind the mask with an interesting story to tell.

THE DETECTIVE

I'm Dr. Joseph Bell, a Scottish medical professor who can figure out your occupation and even what's wrong with you before I hear a word about your symptoms. Of course, I'm no magician, just very observant. Indeed, my acute powers of deduction partly inspired Sir Arthur Conan Doyle when he invented the famous fictional detective Sherlock Holmes.

THE MASTER OF DISGUISE

Major Richard Hannay, the hero of John Buchan's spy story *The 39 Steps*, was based on me, Scottish soldier Edmund Ironside. During the Second Boer War (1899–1902) in South Africa, I disguised myself as an ox-cart driver to spy on the German authorities who controlled South West Africa. I did such a good job that I was given a medal by my German enemies!

THE PLAYBOY

The writer Ian Fleming based James Bond on yours truly, Sidney Reilly. I spied for Britain during World War I, and later hatched a plan to assassinate Vladimir Lenin, the Soviet leader. A master of disguise and a gifted linguist, I'm also a crack shot and a big hit with the ladies. Eat your heart out, 007!

THE SPYMASTER

William Melville's the name, but I sign all my spy documents "M"... and yes, James Bond's boss "M" was named after me. As the "Godfather of MI5," I got Harry Houdini—the famous escape artist—to show my agents how to pick locks and vanish into thin air. In the field, I liked to snoop around disguised as a health inspector.

THE TECH GURU

Bond's tech expert "Q" may be a whizz with gadgets, but long before he hit the silver screen, my Sidcot Suit—named after me, Sidney Cotton—kept the Red Baron (the ace German fighter pilot) and other World War I pilots warm in their chilly cockpits. Later, I invented new ways of taking sneaky spy photos from the air, even taking snapshots of German military airports in 1939, just before World War II.

MISSION: IMPROBABLE

Looking for the strangest spy stories ever told? These tales are out of this world—from experiments with remote-controlled animals to pigeon-brained schemes to blow up battleships.

CONTROL FREAK

In the 1960s, Spanish doctor José Delgado was part of Project Pandora—a CIA experiment into mind control, which fired microwaves at subjects' brains to see how they would affect mood and behavior. Dr. Delgado also

planted wires in bulls' brains and aimed radio signals at them. He made one bull charge, stop, turn right, and charge again—just by pressing a button on a remote control. It is rumored that he has carried out similar experiments on humans!

THE PSYCHIC SQUAD

Gleb Bokiy, head of the "Special Department" with responsibility for protecting Soviet state secrets, was also Russia's spook-master. Bokiy certainly thought outside the box—he sent agents on missions to spot flying saucers, used a "black room" to carry out research into ghosts, and ate raw dog flesh to improve his health. In the 1930s, his mind-control techniques were tested by Soviet leader Joseph Stalin to see whose minds were plotting against him!

BEAM IT OVER, SCOTTIE?

Chinese scientists are currently trying to create completely spy-proof forms of communication. They are attempting to make gifted adults and children teleport matter using brain power alone. If it works, a message written by a general at headquarters would immediately appear on the desks of his officers on the front line, and be impossible to intercept!

FOWL PLAY?

It's World War II and the U.S. Navy wants to blow up a German battleship—who do they call? Behavior expert B.F. Skinner of course. Skinner placed a camera on the front of a missile, linked to a screen inside it. He then popped in a pigeon, specially trained to read the screen and recognize if the missile strayed off course. If so, the bird had been taught to peck at the screen to guide the missile back on target.

A DATE WITH DESTINY

During World War II, MI5 got very excited about the prospect of getting inside the mind of Nazi leader Adolf Hitler. Top astrologer Louis de Wohl convinced them that, since the Führer loved to read his horoscope and was influenced by the stars, he was likely to choose a "lucky" astrological date for his next big operation.

OPERATION NORTHWOODS

In 1962, Cuban leader Fidel Castro was at the top of the CIA's most-wanted list. So the CIA hatched a plan to carry out terrorist acts on American cities that they could then blame on the Cubans. Bombings, phony riots, hijackings, sabotage—the works—all to justify sending a massive U.S. invasion force Fidel's way. Who knows, it could have worked if President John F. Kennedy hadn't vetoed the operation.

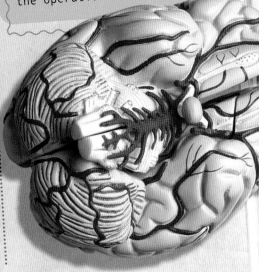

DEATH RAY

In the 1930s, Nazi agents spread the rumor that German scientists were building a "Sun Gun"—a giant mirror in space that could fry an entire city using radio waves. British scientist Robert Watson-Watt was asked if a death ray could work. "No," he replied, "but radio waves might be used to spot a plane..." His assistant proved him right and radar was born.

ZOMBIE ASSASSINS?

Project Bluebird was the brainchild of CIA scientist Dr. Sidney Gottlieb. In the 1950s, his team carried out mind-control experiments on American soldiers using powerful mind-altering drugs. Nasty stuff, but the story that the CIA was trying to create an army of zombie assassins was dead on its feet.

NEW WORLD ORDER

Powerful, secretive groups are plotting to rule mankind with a single government, known as the New World Order (NWO). They control spy agencies such as the CIA, as well as the United Nations... or so say the conspiracy-mongers. The evidence they cite for this Big Brother world? Such things as closed-circuit cameras, bar codes, and DNA testing.

CONSPIRACY THEORIES

When something shocking happens, it's not long before the conspiracy theorists come up with a secret plot or two, and who better to accuse than the nearest spy agency? On the other hand, what better way for a spy agency to get the upper hand over a rival agency than by spinning a web of lies about them? The world is rife with plots, schemes, and conspiracies, but believing in them is just plain paranoid... or is it?

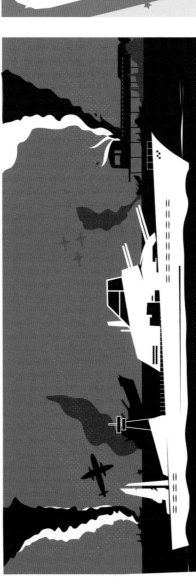

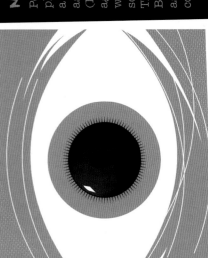

PEARL HARBOR ATTACK

Some conspiracy theorists believe that, in 1941, British prime minister Winston Churchill deliberately failed to tell President Roosevelt about a likely Japanese attack on Pearl Harbor—an attack that brought the United States into World War II. Although the charge is probably untrue, British agents did suspect a sneak attack, but they thought the Philippines or Malaya would be the target.

BLACK PROPAGANDA

The KGB loved spreading rumors to make America look bad. During the 1980s, Moscow radio spread the "news" that 170 children from Central America had been sent to the United States, where their body parts were used to save sick children. Several other radio stations repeated the story before they realized it was a big fat lie!

9/11 CONSPIRACY

A popular conspiracy theory suggests that U.S. intelligence agencies knew about the terrorist attacks on New York's Twin Towers on September 11, 2001, but allowed them to go ahead. Why? To provide a reason for the United States to go to war in the oil-rich Middle East. Conspiracy theorists also suggest that, in return, the agencies received extra funding and powers from the U.S. government for the resulting "War on Terror" campaign.

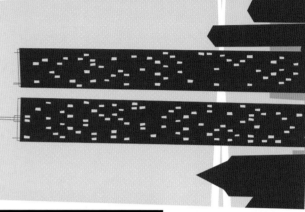

WHO SHOT JFK?

Some say that the CIA was behind the 1963 assassination of President John F. Kennedy, after they clashed over the agency's failed attempt to overthrow the Cuban Communist government. Other theories point to the Soviet KGB, since Lee Harvey Oswald—the man who pulled the trigger—had briefly defected to the Soviet Union four years earlier.

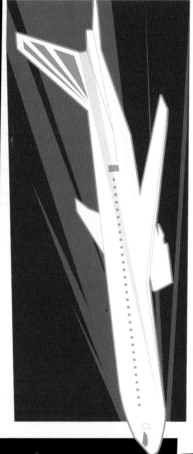

FRYING YOUR BRAIN

In the 1990s, the High Frequency Active Auroral Research Program (HAARP) in Alaska was a secret project to build a super-powerful radio transmitter that could communicate with submarines in deep waters. It's been blamed for freak weather all over the world, and some fear that the intense beam of radio waves could fry people's brains!

A SPY PLANE?

On September 1, 1983, Soviet fighters shot down a Korean Airlines passenger plane over the Sea of Japan, killing all 269 passengers and crew members on board. No bodies were ever found. This has led to a number of conspiracy theories. Was it actually a U.S. spy plane? And did Soviet mini-subs secretly snatch the evidence? These questions remain unanswered...

MIND HACKING

In 1996, a team of scientists announced that by 2025, there would be microchips that could record everything you thought, felt, or experienced. It wasn't long before rumors circulated that the CIA was working hard to develop just such a chip—known as the "Soul Catcher"—which would allow them to hack into people's minds!

SPY WARS

War is a time when people at the top have a lot of secrets, making spying a top priority. Good intelligence makes all the difference in the heat of battle, while well-placed moles and devious double agents can create chaos behind enemy lines. From the ancient Sumerian smoke-signaling spies to the covert code breakers of World War II, spies are the key to being on the winning side.

SECRETS OF THE ANCIENTS

Spying is as old as war, and ancient spies were just as brave, ruthless, and cunning as today's secret agents. In fact, you can still learn a thing or two by digging up some sneaky spy tricks from the past....

1 SMOKE SIGNALS

In 3200 BCE, the ancient Sumerians scratched out intelligence reports on stone and clay tablets. As you can imagine, it wasn't the speediest way to deliver a vital message. But Sumerian spies inside the city of Babylon (now in Iraq) had a bright idea: using smoke signals to send information about the city's defenses back to their own lines.

2 A SECRET FORMULA

A Sumerian tablet used one of the world's first known ciphers. Why use code? The Sumerians were very proud of the glaze that made their pots so special, and the tablet warned that spies from other civilizations were out to steal the formula, which had to be guarded at all costs.

3 SNOOPER TROOPERS

Around 800 BCE, the Assyrians set out to conquer the known world. Leading the way were mounted scouts acting as the eyes and ears of their awesome army. Meanwhile, the world's first secret police, known as the "King's Messengers," snooped on rebels and other troublemakers within the Assyrian empire.

4 HAIR RAID

The Bible recounts the story of Samson—an Israelite with God-given strength who slayed the Philistines by the thousands. In order to find the secret of his strength, Philistine spies bribed the beautiful Delilah, who Samson was in love with. Discovering it was his hair, she had a servant cut off his curls while he snoozed. The Philistine spies who were hiding in her house then bound the weakened Samson's hands and feet, gouged out his eyes, and smuggled him to their temple for imprisonment.

5 CODE RED

Before attacking Jericho, the Jewish leader Joshua sent two spies into the city to check its military strength. They managed to persuade the local innkeeper, Rahab, to hide them. When Jericho guards came to question Rahab, she hid the spies under bundles of flax on the roof. In return for her help, the spies gave her a scarlet thread as a marker so her family would be spared in the coming attack.

6 HORSE PLAY

In a classic piece of deception, legend has it that the ancient Greek army acted out a mock defeat and presented a huge wooden horse to the city of Troy as a symbol of their victory. As the Greek warriors secretly lay in wait inside the horse, a small group of Greek warriors pretended to sail back to Greece, only to emerge that night and open the city's gates to let the rest of the Greek army in, and finally capture Troy.

7 RUNAWAY RUSE

The Persian king Cyrus the Great (576–530 BCE) led a bloody revolt against the ruling Medes—an ancient Iranian people—and conquered their empire. One of his tactics was to send out spies disguised as runaway slaves. With their clanking chains, they convinced the Medes that they wanted to betray their former master, but all the while, they were actually feeding them false information about Cyrus and his plans.

8 DO THE TWIST

Around 500 BCE, the warlike Spartans invented the scytale—a cunning but simple device that was an early form of cryptography. They wrote a message on a narrow strip of parchment that had been wound around a thin rod. Unwinding the scroll broke up the letters of the message. When it reached its destination, the strip was wound around a rod of the same width to unscramble the text.

9 PASS ON THE MESSAGE

Ancient Greek spymasters hid messages inside earrings and sandals. They also created the first hydraulic telegraph system, which allowed messages to be sent over long distances. According to the ancient Greek historian Polybius, it was first used in the First Punic War (264–241 BCE) between Sicily and Carthage.

Marco Polo
(c. 1254–1324)
You may have heard that I'm a bit of a traveler extraordinaire... In 1271, I trekked across Asia on a secret mission for the rulers of Venice, Italy. Once in China, I won the trust of Mongol leader Kublai Khan, who offered me a job as ambassador— the perfect cover for a traveling spy!

Edward I
(1239–1307)
Who goes there? By command of King Edward I, all unknown travelers entering a city from dusk until dawn are to be locked up and handed to the sheriff. I like to be sure that I'm not on the receiving end of a spy mission, although I do use spies myself: In 1305, I defeated rebels in Scotland after a servant betrayed the rebel leader William Wallace.

Mongol soldier
All hail Genghis Khan (1162–1227), lord of the mighty Mongols! Disguised as a merchant, I, a Mongol spy, learn a lot from travelers, traders, and pilgrims, who are all too happy to accept some gold coinage in return for info! Changing horses every 28 miles (45 km) or so means I can ride 186 miles (300 km) in a day to bring Genghis the hottest news.

Never trust a traveler

Take a trek through medieval times, but be warned—merchants, ambassadors, and traveling singers are not always who or what they seem. These wily operators maintain double lives as spies and informers, and will use many an underhand tactic to wheedle out any information they can.

Alfred the Great
(849–899 CE)
I'm no wandering minstrel but king of the Saxons! Disguise is my secret weapon against the Vikings, who are all over England like a bad smell. Upon seeing my harp, they'll welcome me into their camp and, with a song in their hearts and beer in their bellies, never fail to tell all and reveal their battle plans!

BEYOND THE BARRICADES

Over the years, countless rebel groups have used spy tactics in their efforts to force invaders out of their homeland. Many of the rebels were already in secret organizations with their own signs, disguises, and passwords. Others were ordinary workers willing to sacrifice their lives for freedom.

The spies who weren't

During the buildup to World War I, rabble-rousing books and films terrified the British public into thinking their country was crawling with enemy spies. Many were suspected, including anarchists who staged antigovernment riots and launched attacks on police and politicians.

Liberty or death!

During the American Revolution, around 30 U.S. patriots formed a secret spy group called the "Mechanics." In 1776, one of them, Nathan Hale, bravely volunteered to go behind enemy lines and spy on British defenses near New York. But with little training, no contacts, and no cover story, he was soon captured and executed.

Wake-up call

On November 21, 1920, Irish rebel leader Michael Collins carried out early-morning raids against the British agents (above) sent to Dublin to spy on his men. Of the 60 or so agents, 19 were shot dead after moles inside British headquarters in Dublin passed on their details.

Simply patriotic

Cross-eyed patriot Nancy Morgan Hart was so good at acting like a simpleton that she simply strolled into British camps in Georgia during the American Revolution to gather information. After the war, six loyalist soldiers broke into her house; she captured them, killing two, then hanged the others when her husband arrived home.

Viva Mexico!

In 1865, American general Phil Sheridan began arming a Mexican rebellion against the country's French emperor, Maximilian. A year later, U.S. agents seized a letter showing that France wanted to abandon the emperor, so Sheridan sent the rebels even more guns. The French pulled out, and Maximilian faced a firing squad.

Get the message?

While fighting Napoleon in Spain, the Duke of Wellington used Spanish guerillas to help him capture French messengers. At first, they just brought the messenger's heads! But in July 1812, they handed him a coded report, allowing him to decipher the French battle plans. *Olé!*

The bullet factory

In 1945, when the British army left Palestine, Jewish freedom fighters feared that they wouldn't be able to defend themselves against an Arab invasion. In less than a month, they built a secret bullet factory hidden beneath a laundromat, and a team of 50 workers produced two million bullets in just three years.

FEMMES FATALES

Don't be fooled by their feigned innocence, Mr. Checkpoint Guard—there's been a long line of steely female spies throughout the ages. Some craved action, hiding daggers in their petticoats or blowing bridges to kingdom come. Others fluttered their eyelashes to extract secrets from men in high places, or to slip quietly behind enemy lines.

THE WILD ROSE

Southern belle Rose Greenhow was invited to all the best parties in Washington, D.C., where she charmed Union officials into telling their secrets during the Civil War. But in 1861, Union spymaster Allan Pinkerton found military maps in her home, and "Wild Rose" was locked up for spying.

THE CHARMER

Staunch Confederate Belle Boyd was quite the charmer, flashing a smile to get herself out of any pickle—and to extract military secrets from Union officer Daniel Keily in 1861. She conveyed this intelligence to Confederate officers via her slave, who carried messages in a hollowed-out watch case.

HELPING HAND

During the Civil War, wealthy Southerner Elizabeth Van Lew brought food and medicine to Union prisoners at a nearby Confederate prison—and helped them escape. Hoping to end slavery in the South, she also smuggled important intelligence about the Confederate army gleaned from her loyal subagents.

BRAVE SLAVE

An escaped slave, Harriet Tubman disguised herself as a poor farmer's wife during the Civil War to spy on the Confederate army. Under the cover of darkness, she also led other escaped slaves from one safe house to another along secret "underground" routes to freedom in the Union states.

ONE-LEGGED WONDER

U.S. agent Virginia Hall was at the top of the Nazis' most-wanted list after masterminding many raids by French Resistance fighters during World War II—despite having a wooden leg. This queen of disguises learned how to walk without a limp and once dressed as a milkmaid to evade Nazi attempts to capture her.

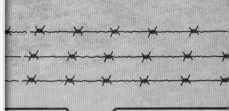

HOLY STATUES

During World War I, German spy Maria de Victoria seemed unusually fond of her silk scarves. When British agents caught her, they found invisible ink in one scarf and a reappearing chemical in another. They also discovered a dastardly plot to smuggle explosives into the United States in hollow statues of the Virgin Mary.

THE WHITE MOUSE

In 1943, to replace a lost code, Australian spy Nancy Wake rode a bicycle 62 miles (100 km) through a string of German checkpoints. She also reputedly killed an SS sentry with her bare hands to stop him from raising the alarm. No wonder the Gestapo offered five million francs to catch the spy they called the "White Mouse."

MY LIPS ARE SEALED

In June 1944, British spy Violette Szabo was sent to France to sabotage German forces as they headed north to fight the Allies. Ambushed by a German patrol, Szabo was shot but gallantly fought on to allow her French comrades to escape. The Gestapo tortured her for weeks but she told them nothing and was executed in 1945.

READY, SET, SPY!

At the start of World War I, most people thought the conflict was going to be a quick sprint to victory. But muddy conditions and poor tactics quickly turned it into a grisly marathon that would last from 1914 to 1918. So another race began—to come up with new gadgets and spy tactics such as wiretapping, code breaking, and intercepting enemy signals. This was vital work. When British code breakers ambushed a German telegram in 1917, its contents would inspire the United States to join the race, and change the course of the war.

Meet the teams

World War I was a battle between the Central Powers and the Allies. The key players for the Central Powers were Germany, Austria-Hungary, and Turkey. The lead Allies were Britain, France, and Russia, joined by the United States in 1917. In all, 28 countries took part, making this the first global war.

1 German spy mistress

The Germans set up spy schools in occupied Belgium, including one run by Elizabeth "Tiger Eyes" Schragmüller, mother of modern spy training. Her students, known only by code names, spent 12 hours a day training, and the rest of it locked in their rooms! If successful, they were sent behind Allied lines.

2 Austrian math team

This was the first war in which spies listened in on each other's radio messages. Austria-Hungary started ahead of the pack, thanks to Max Ronge and his math-genius team. Their work led to a major victory in 1915 after they revealed when and where the Russian army planned to attack.

3 Turkish interrogation

In 1917, Turkish intelligence had a hunch that Jewish spies were working for Britain in Palestine. Their suspicions were confirmed when they intercepted a carrier pigeon. After capturing one spy, the Turks interrogated her under torture until she revealed all, leading to the capture and execution of the entire Jewish spy ring.

4 British breakthrough

In 1917, Room 40, British military intelligence's code-breaking bureau, intercepted and deciphered a telegram sent by the German secretary of state saying that Germany would back a Mexican invasion of the United States. Soon after this information was revealed, America joined the war.

5 American spy catchers

German and Austrian agents carried out more than 50 acts of sabotage in the United States. However, U.S. agents caught several potential saboteurs, including German Werner Horn who, in 1915, had been ordered to dynamite a key U.S. railroad bridge used to ship Canadian soldiers and supplies.

6 French code breaker

In June 1918, the German army was poised to capture Paris and win the war. French code breaker Georges Painvin was given a vital message, in a German code known as ADFGVX, to decrypt. He cracked it and the German attack was beaten back, but Painvin lost 33 lb (15 kg) due to stress.

7 Russian bungler

Russia's radio equipment was so poor that their signals teams had to broadcast battle plans in Morse code, which was known all over the world. As a result, in 1914, German agents were able to draw the Russian army into a trap near Tannenberg (in modern Poland) where they were crushed.

RED ORCHESTRA

During the two world wars, the Communists took a firm grip on Russia, led by Joseph Stalin (1878–1953). Their secret police force, the Cheka, ruthlessly dealt with anyone not in tune with Communism, while their military intelligence unit, the GRU, spread across Europe to counter the threat from Nazi Germany. It formed a vast espionage ring that the Germans nicknamed the "Red Orchestra."

THE CONDUCTOR

Leopold Trepper, the "Big Chief," was one of the GRU's top agents. In 1939, posing as a Canadian industrialist from the made-up Foreign Excellent Raincoat Company, he traveled all over Europe recruiting agents. Within a few months he had nearly 200 spies.

BELGIUM

In early 1939, Leopold Trepper was sent to Belgium. The team of spies that he recruited sent regular radio messages to Moscow from a transmitter on the top floor of a house in Brussels. But they had to face the music when the Gestapo (Nazi secret police) shut them down in December 1941.

FRANCE

In 1940, Trepper moved to Paris. His French unit provided intelligence to Resistance fighters and tapped the phones of the German army intelligence headquarters. After selling black-market goods to the Germans, Trepper was arrested by the Gestapo in December 1942. He later escaped and went into hiding with the French Resistance.

GERMANY

Trepper's aims struck a chord with more than a dozen anti-Nazi citizens based in Berlin, including lawyer Arvid Harnack, air-force intelligence officer Harro Schulze-Boysen, and Horst Heilmann—an officer in the German army headquarters. They passed secret documents to the Soviets until they were caught, and executed in 1942.

THE PIANISTS

Referred to as "pianists" by the Germans, the Red Orchestra's radio operators reported to Moscow. But their intelligence wasn't always music to the ears of Russia's Soviet leader, Joseph Stalin, who was paranoid about double agents, and in 1941 he hit a wrong note when he ignored the pianists' rumors of a German invasion.

THE PIANOS

Just four days after the German invasion of Russia in May 1941, the radios, or "pianos" as the Germans called them, used by Trepper's agents in Germany failed. His "pianists" were forced to rely on human couriers, who were much more likely to be intercepted.

SWITZERLAND

After Trepper's arrest in 1942, the Soviets increasingly relied on a GRU unit known as the Red Three, based in neutral Switzerland. This was led by Alexander Rado, code name "Dora," who had useful contacts inside Germany. Rado set up a radio transmitter high in the Swiss Alps, so the signal was as clear as a bell in Moscow!

THE LUCY RING

The Red Three unit often played second fiddle to the Lucy Ring run by Rudolf Roessler in Lucerne, Switzerland. This provided some of the best intelligence about German operations against the Soviets, thanks to moles such as Lieutenant General Fritz Theile—a senior officer in the German army's communications unit.

THE SABOTEUR'S TOOL KIT

World War II began in 1939 when Germany invaded Poland. It lasted for six years and involved 61 countries, mainly split across two sides: the Axis, including Germany, Italy, and Japan; and the Allies, including Britain, the United States, France, and Australia. Working deep inside enemy lines, secret agents from both sides used every trick in the book to swing things in their favor. They became expert saboteurs, using a surprising mix of tools to do the job.

1. Limpet mine

These cunning devices used magnets to stick onto the metal side of a ship, just like a limpet clings to a rock. In September 1943, 14 Australian and British commandos from Z Force canoed into Singapore Harbor and attached limpet mines to Japanese ships, blowing up seven of them.

2. Fishy banknotes

A Nazi officer planned to disrupt the British economy by flooding the country with forged bills. His team of counterfeiters, mostly Jews from concentration camps, produced some of the finest forgeries ever made. But a British spy learned of the plot and informed the Bank of England.

3. Liberator pistol

Nicknamed the "Woolworth gun" since it was so cheap to make, the Liberator pistol was made by the U.S. military for resistance fighters in occupied countries. Although it came with comic strip instructions, it was no joke. Accurate only to a short range of 26 ft (8 m), its role was to capture a better weapon from an enemy.

4. Lock picking

Picking a lock is an easy way to get ahold of secret material, but it's a real skill. So British naval intelligence whizz Ian Fleming recruited some professional thieves to steal the latest German aircraft engines, and expert safecrackers to break into foreign embassies to steal their codes and ciphers.

5. Hand grenades

A hand grenade lobbed into a movie theater would certainly make people panic. That was a tactic used by Japanese secret agents in British-run Hong Kong to spread fear among the local Chinese (although no one was killed). They added to the mayhem by destroying British army barracks, train sheds, and water pipes.

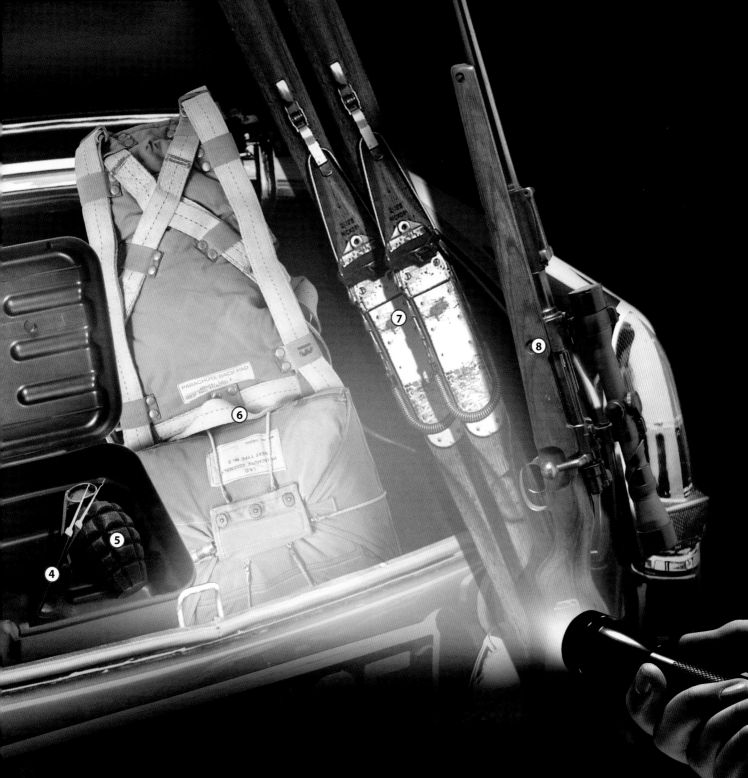

6. Parachute

Perfect for dropping in unannounced behind enemy lines, parachutes were used in the buildup to D-Day in June 1944, when nearly 300 American, British, and French agents dropped into France. Working with the French Resistance, they launched a stunningly effective guerrilla campaign against the Germans.

7. Skis

If it's snowing outside, reach for your skis. Early in 1943, six Norwegian commandos destroyed a German factory that was a key part of the Nazi nuclear weapons program. With 3,000 German soldiers hot on their heels, they escaped by skiing cross-country 250 miles (400 km) to neutral Sweden.

8. Sniper rifle

A rifle with telescopic sights can't be beat when your target is a VIP ringed by guards. It was the number one choice for a British plan to assassinate Hitler in July 1944. It never got the green light, though, partly because some generals believed he was such a bad military commander that he wouldn't be in power for long.

The One That GOT AWAY

SOME SPIES TRADE SECRETS FOR CASH, WHILE OTHERS LOVE THE THRILL OF A DANGEROUS JOB... BUT ENGELBERT BRODA QUIETLY DID WHAT HE THOUGHT WAS RIGHT. BORN IN AUSTRIA IN 1910, HE WAS HANDSOME AND CLEVER. FROM A YOUNG AGE, HE WAS ALSO A COMMUNIST.

DARLING, WHICH TEDDY BEAR DO YOU LIKE BEST?

COMRADE, ALL BEARS ARE EQUAL!

WHEN HE WAS A UNIVERSITY STUDENT, BRODA, OR "BERTIE" AS HE WAS KNOWN TO HIS FRIENDS, WAS ARRESTED AND THEN IMPRISONED SEVERAL TIMES FOR OPPOSING THE NAZI GERMAN TAKEOVER OF AUSTRIA.

DOWN WITH HITLER! UP WITH STALIN!

IN 1938, AT AGE 28, BRODA FLED TO BRITAIN. HE PRETENDED TO BE AN EAGER SCIENCE STUDENT WHO WAS HOPING TO ATTEND A UNIVERSITY LECTURE IN BRISTOL... BUT BRODA SECRETLY HAD OTHER PLANS.

IF WAR BREAKS OUT, I WONDER HOW I CAN HELP THE COMMUNIST CAUSE...

THE BRITISH INTELLIGENCE AGENCY, MI5, ALREADY HAD THEIR SUSPICIONS ABOUT BRODA—HE HAD LINKS TO A COMMUNIST SPY WHO DIED MYSTERIOUSLY IN VIENNA IN 1931. THEY SOON FOUND OUT THAT BRODA WAS THE LEADER OF A GROUP OF AUSTRIAN COMMUNISTS THAT INCLUDED EDITH TUDOR HART— PHOTOGRAPHER BY DAY, KGB COURIER AND AGENT BY NIGHT.

YOU WORK FOR THE KGB? WOW! WHAT'S YOUR CODE NAME?

EDITH. SHH! DON'T TELL ANYONE.

BRODA WAS SOON RECRUITED BY EDITH INTO THE KGB.

MI5 DID THEIR BEST TO PROVE THAT BRODA WAS A SPY. THEY OPENED HIS MAIL...

WHO SAID SPYING WAS GLAMOROUS?

TAPPED HIS TELEPHONE...

AND FOLLOWED HIM HOME.

IN 1939, MI5 EVEN LOCKED BRODA UP BRIEFLY AND SEARCHED HIS APARTMENT. BUT BRODA WAS CLEAN... OR SO THEY THOUGHT.

EEWW! THAT'S WHAT I CALL CHEMICAL WARFARE!

IN 1941, BRODA WAS STILL DOING HIS SCIENCE THING AND WAS OFFERED A JOB AT THE CAVENDISH LABORATORY IN CAMBRIDGE, WORKING ON ATOMIC REACTORS. WHEN MI5 TRIED TO BLOCK THE APPOINTMENT, IT WAS OVERRULED: IT WAS MORE IMPORTANT TO BEAT THE NAZIS IN THE RACE TO BUILD A NUCLEAR BOMB.

WE'RE CONCERNED ABOUT BRODA.

DON'T WORRY, WE WON'T SHOW HIM ANY OF THE REALLY SECRET STUFF.

BUT BRODA DID SEE THE SECRET STUFF. IN CAMBRIDGE, HE WORKED ALONGSIDE HANS VON HALBAN, ONE OF THE WORLD'S TOP NUCLEAR SCIENTISTS.

WANNA KNOW THE SECRET OF NUCLEAR POWER?

DO TELL!

BRODA, CODE-NAMED "ERIC" BY THE KGB, WAS SOON AT THE HEART OF THE MANHATTAN PROJECT—THE JOINT BRITISH AND AMERICAN SCIENTIFIC PROGRAM TO DEVELOP THE FIRST ATOMIC BOMB. WITHIN ONE YEAR, HE WAS PASSING ON SECRETS TO THE KGB VIA EDITH.

THIS IS PRETTY EXPLOSIVE STUFF!

THE KGB COULDN'T BELIEVE THEIR LUCK. BRODA HAD THE POTENTIAL TO BECOME A KEY PART OF THEIR PLAN, CODE-NAMED "ENORMOUS," TO STEAL NUCLEAR SECRETS FROM BRITAIN AND AMERICA.

замечательный!

невероятный!

AND HE DIDN'T EVEN WANT TO BE PAID!

THE KGB ASKED EDITH TO ARRANGE A MEETING BETWEEN THIS EAGER NEW RECRUIT AND THEIR MAN IN LONDON, CODE-NAMED "GLAN." BRODA AGREED TO HAND OVER ANY ATOMIC SECRETS HE COULD LAY HIS HANDS ON, INCLUDING ALL THE FILES SENT OVER FROM THE UNITED STATES.

WHAT "CANDY" CAN YOU GIVE ME?

I CAN GET AHOLD OF JELLY BEANS, LICORICE STICKS, AND THE LATEST GUMDROPS FROM AMERICA.

MEANWHILE, THE NET WAS CLOSING. BY 1943, MI5 HAD PLANTED ITS OWN MOLE, CODE-NAMED "KASPAR," AMONG THE AUSTRIAN COMMUNISTS LIVING IN BRITAIN.

HMM. WHATEVER HE KNOWS, SO DOES SHE.

FROM 1942 TO 1945, BRODA WAS TRAVELING TO LONDON FROM CAMBRIDGE UP TO THREE TIMES A WEEK. HE MARKED A PAGE IN A PHONE BOOK IN A PARTICULAR PHONE BOOTH TO LET HIS HANDLERS KNOW HE WAS READY TO TALK.

KGB AGENTS WOULD GO TO THE PHONE BOOTH AND, SEEING THE MARK, WOULD KNOW TO MEET BRODA AT AN AGREED-UPON TIME AND PLACE.

I'M NERVOUS MEETING YOU IN PERSON.

NO NEED FOR A DEAD DROP. THOSE MI5-SKIS ARE IDIOTS!

BRODA ALSO PASSED INFORMATION THROUGH HIS DENTIST, A RUSSIAN NAMED SCHKOLNIKOFF.

WHAT NEWS THIS WEEK?

NNNGH, NNGH, NNNGAHH.

BY LATE 1943, BRODA WAS WORKING ON THE "TUBE ALLOYS" PROJECT— THE CODE NAME FOR BRITISH NUCLEAR WEAPON RESEARCH INTO THE USE OF PLUTONIUM, THE VITAL INGREDIENT USED IN THE ATOMIC BOMB. ITS VERY EXISTENCE WAS TOP SECRET.

TUBE ALLOYS

TOTALLY TOP SECRET

THE ALARM BELLS STARTED RINGING FOR BRODA WHEN A FELLOW KGB SPY, ALAN NUNN MAY, WAS ARRESTED IN 1946. BRODA KEPT HIS COOL AND SECRETLY PLANNED HIS ESCAPE. HE LEFT BRITAIN FOR A "SHORT HOLIDAY"—AND NEVER CAME BACK AGAIN.

ANYTHING TO DECLARE?

JUST A TUBE OF ALLOYS... I MEAN SUNSCREEN.

BY 1948, BRODA WAS BACK IN AUSTRIA AS A UNIVERSITY LECTURER IN VIENNA. HE REMAINED THERE FOR THE REST OF HIS LIFE. HE DIED IN 1983, AT AGE 73, A HIGHLY RESPECTED SCIENTIST. AND FOR ALL THEIR EFFORTS, MI5 NEVER DID CATCH UP WITH BRODA.

HOWEVER, IN THE 1990S, JOURNALIST ALEXANDER VASSILIEV WAS ALLOWED A PEEK AT SECRET KGB FILES (NOW SEALED), AND UNCOVERED BRODA'S SECRET IDENTITY.

P.S., I'M ERIC!

BRODA 1910 - 1983

IT ALSO REVEALED HIS ROLE IN CREATING THE FIRST SOVIET NUCLEAR BOMB IN 1949— A TRIGGER FOR THE COLD WAR BETWEEN THE SOVIET UNION AND THE UNITED STATES.

BATTLE OF THE MOLES

In 1949, the Soviet Union exploded its first atomic bomb, starting an arms race with the United States. For the next 40 years, the world was on tenterhooks, fearing nuclear war. The conflict never reached that lethal boiling point, however, so it started to be called the Cold War. But an underground spy battle raged as moles were planted on both sides to dig up secrets.

HOT SECRETS

German-born British physicist Klaus Fuchs was a KGB mole who was working on the U.S. nuclear program, the Manhattan Project. Fuchs handed over nuclear secrets to the Soviets, but spilled the beans to the British in 1950 when he was outed by code-breaking Operation Venona.

MR. AND MRS. SPY

KGB spies Julius and Ethel Rosenberg passed on secrets about U.S. military technology to the Soviets. The husband-and-wife team was arrested in 1950 following the West's success at cracking a Soviet cipher during Operation Venona. They were the only American civilians executed for spying in the Cold War.

CAUGHT ON FILM

West German politician Alfred Frenzel had a Communist past that the Czech intelligence service (StB) used to blackmail him into working for them in 1956. They gave him the code name "Anna" and a big payoff for film of top secret documents smuggled in cans of talcum powder and a statue rigged with explosives. Frenzel was arrested in 1960.

CODE NAME: TOP HAT

Recruited in 1960, Major General Dmitri Polyakov was a top U.S. mole inside Soviet intelligence. He handed over details of Soviet antitank missiles and four KGB moles. To signal his handlers, he rode a streetcar past the U.S. embassy and activated a transmitter, but Top Hat's cover was blown by mole Aldrich Ames in 1988.

THE SUPERMOLE

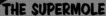

In 1961, U.S. counterintelligence boss James Angleton was alerted by a former KGB spy to supposed Soviet plans to plant a supermole inside the CIA. Part of the plan was apparently to send a fake defector, so when Yuri Nosenko defected to the United States, he was locked up for three years while CIA agents tried to get him to confess. Meanwhile, Angleton's witch hunt tore the CIA apart, but the supermole, if he ever existed, was never found.

YOU'VE BEEN FRAMED

During the 1970s and 1980s, the CIA planted many moles inside the Cuban intelligence agency (DGI). Or so it thought... In 1987, a source revealed that most of the moles were double agents planted by the DGI. To rub it in, Cuban state television showed the "moles" explaining how they had tricked the CIA.

AGENTS FOR CASH

In the 1980s, CIA staffer Aldrich Ames revealed the names of all the U.S. spies in the Soviet Union, leading to the deaths of at least 10 agents. In return, the KGB paid him about $4.6 million. A colleague noticed that Ames was living large and, in 1994, the FBI swooped in and Ames was arrested.

BIN BAG SECRETS

Over 17 years to 1991, FBI agent Robert Hanssen received cash from the Soviets in return for classified documents dropped off in bin bags, and the names of several U.S. moles. Foolishly, Hanssen kept digital copies of these documents on his PalmPilot. After downloading the files, the FBI arrested Hanssen, who confessed all, asking, "What took you so long?"

THE WALL COMES DOWN

Built in 1961, the Berlin Wall dividing East and West Germany symbolized the Cold War between the democratic United States and its allies in the West, and the Communist Soviet Union. In the 1980s, the American strategy to bring down the Soviets led to intelligence operations of sabotage, propaganda, and the support of rebel groups. As the Soviet Union struggled with the cost of being a superpower, the KGB was crumbling. In 1989, the Berlin Wall came down, and the following year Germany was reunified. The Cold War was almost over.

Carrot and stick

Soviet citizens visiting the West—whether sailors, tourists, officials, or athletes—were sometimes met by agents handing out anti-Communist newspapers in the Russian language, which they might risk smuggling back to the Soviet Union. More hardcore methods were used by the NTS—a Russian anti-Communist resistance movement set up back in the 1930s—which tried to recruit Russians as spies, using blackmail or bribery if necessary.

Hey, big spender

In 1981, backed by the president and Congress, new CIA boss William J. Casey launched an ingenious covert operation—supporting guerrilla groups across the world in their fight against the Communists! Operation Cyclone spent billions of dollars to arm Afghan rebels, who eventually drove the Soviets out of Afghanistan. The CIA paid to equip anti-Communist "freedom fighters" from Africa to Central America with arms, supplies, and even high-tech antiaircraft missiles.

The art of persuasion

Western spies bombarded Eastern Europe with anti-Soviet propaganda leaflets, which were cunningly blown in on the wind attached to balloons, or floated downstream in watertight packages. Anti-Soviet books were also distributed, with the CIA funding hundreds of propaganda-filled titles, and even an animated film version of George Orwell's anti-Communist novel *Animal Farm*.

Straight talking

Originally funded by the CIA, but with a policy of unbiased reporting, Radio Free Europe and Radio Liberty blitzed Russian and Eastern European airwaves with round-the-clock transmissions. They sparked the overthrow of the Communist government in Czechoslovakia in 1989, when their (inaccurate) reports that a student had been killed by police led to huge demonstrations.

Winning the war in the air

The CIA spent big bucks on moles and defectors to try and bring the Soviet Union down from within. In the early 1980s, electronics engineer and Soviet defector Adolf Georgievich Tolkachev used matchbox-sized cameras to copy secret files on the Soviets' latest aircraft radars. The CIA paid him $200,000 a year for his intelligence, until Soviet mole Aldrich Ames betrayed him, leading to his execution as a spy in 1986.

руб

Rise of the profiteers

By the 1980s, the Soviet Union was struggling to pay its bills. Russian trade organizations paid bribes of thousands of rubles to get laws passed in their favor, which allowed them to sell scarce goods at a huge profit. The KGB did its best to fight corruption, but its investigation merely showed the rest of the world how messed up the Soviet economy was.

Peaceful revolution

In 1980, CIA officers began meeting in secret with the Polish trade union Solidarity, which hoped to achieve a "peaceful revolution" in Communist-run Poland. On December 12, 1981, Polish government troops began to round up and imprison thousands of Solidarity members, but the CIA had been warned by a Polish colonel and they managed to hide some.

The revolting KGB

Unhappy with the reforms of Soviet president Gorbachev, KGB officials launched a coup on August 19, 1991. It collapsed in just three days. The chief conspirators (the "Gang of Eight") were arrested, and the KGB was stripped of its military units. The coup led to the breakup of the Soviet Union—the very thing the rebels were trying to prevent.

Software secrets

In 1980, disillusioned KGB colonel Vladimir Vetrov handed 4,000 secret documents to the French spy agency DST, which gave him the code name Farewell. The documents revealed a network of KGB agents (called "Line X") trying to get their hands on Western technology. The CIA obliged by selling them faulty hardware, including one device that caused a major gas pipeline explosion in the Soviet Union.

SPYING TODAY

Advances in technology can be both a help and a hindrance to today's spies. With cyber attacks becoming the new weapons of mass destruction, the digital world poses a very real threat, and modern espionage requires spies to constantly adapt, using a mixed tool bag of traditional techniques and up-to-the-minute technology to keep one step ahead in the spy game.

CHANGING THREATS

Following the end of the Cold War, Western intelligence agencies faced a problem: After dealing with large-scale hostile entities like the Soviet Union for so long, they now found themselves unprepared for a new and unpredictable breed of threats. A former CIA director compared these new threats to a bewildering array of poisonous snakes that had been let loose in a dark jungle.

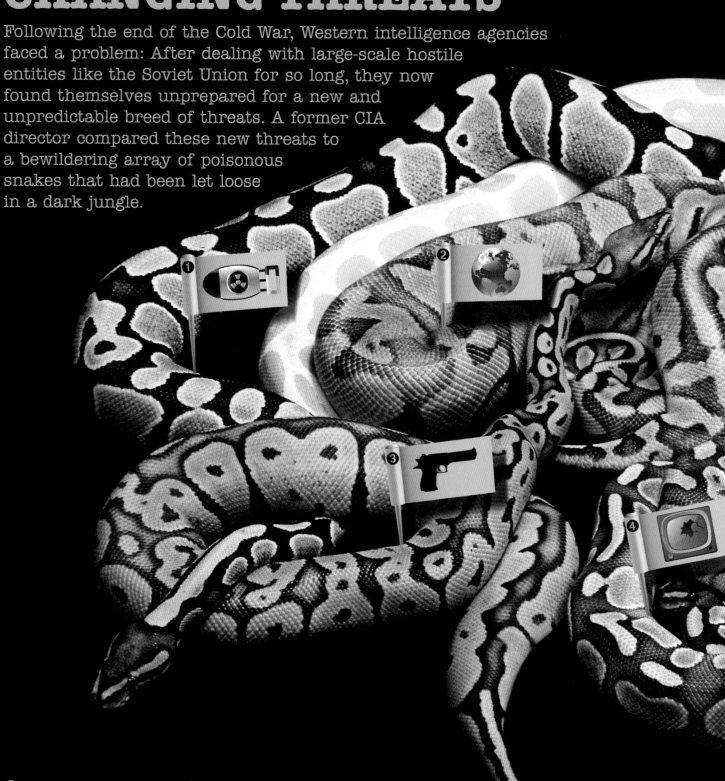

❶ WMDs
Weapons of mass destruction (WMDs) first slithered onto the global stage during World War I, but rocket technology allowed them to become a truly global threat. Today, many countries possess the technology to manufacture nuclear, chemical, or biological devices, and those who can't can buy them on the black market. Monitoring WMD programs is now a top priority for intelligence agencies.

❷ Globalization
In ancient times, threats to national security were mostly confined within a country's borders, but the advent of jet travel, the Internet, and global networking means that a threat can come from anywhere. Today, terrorist networks span the globe, and thanks to the Internet, TV, and radio, their messages can reach anywhere in the world.

❸ Terrorism
What would launch the most effective attack—an elephant or a snake? The elephant may be more powerful, but the snake can take you by surprise. Threats to national security are just the same: Attacks on a country used to only come from another country, which is big and easy to see coming. But today's terrorist attacks can come from any direction and in any form, hidden like a snake in the grass.

❹ Lack of communication
In the wild, meerkats use their numbers to protect their nests from marauding snakes—it really pays to have lots of lookouts to warn you of possible danger. Before the terrorist attacks of September 11, U.S. intelligence had many eyes looking for threats, but the different agencies didn't effectively communicate with each other, so they didn't "see" the imminent threat until it was too late.

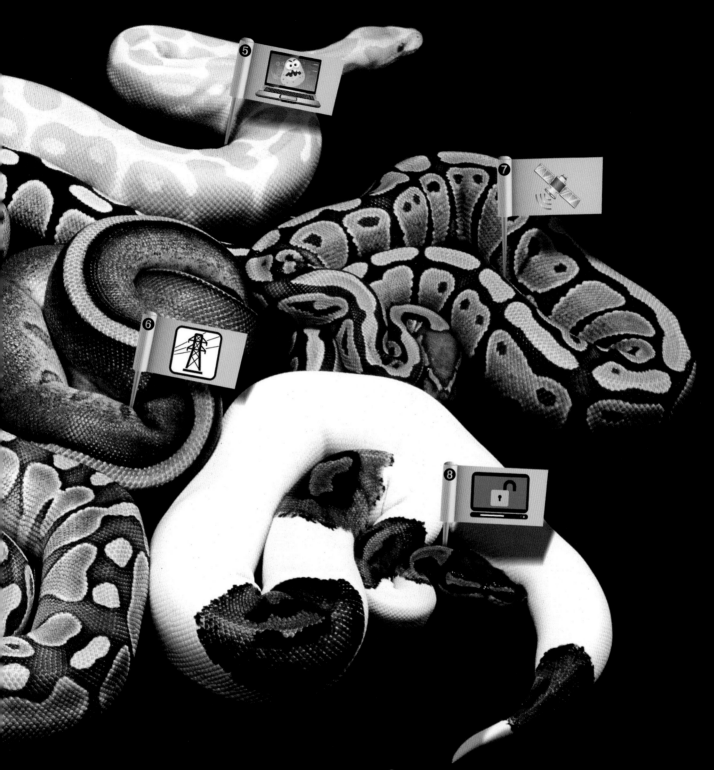

⑤ Cyber attacks

Computers and the Internet have made gathering intelligence and spreading information much easier, but this digital world has also opened up avenues of attack that didn't exist before: Cyber attacks can target military and civilian infrastructures. Around 120 countries now use the Internet for web-espionage operations, and in 2008 alone there were 5,499 breaches of U.S. government computers.

⑥ Future cyber attacks

The security systems protecting some of our vital infrastructures have been criticized as being inadequate. If left unchecked, cyber attackers would be able to wreak havoc in our computer networks. It has been predicted that by 2015 there will be a major cyber attack on the West's power grids, which could plunge its electricity-dependent societies into chaos.

⑦ Reliance on technology

Technology is an incredibly effective tool in the fight against terror, but it pays not to become too reliant on it. Satellites and signals intelligence have made the process of intelligence gathering very efficient, but human spies will always be needed on the ground. After all, you can spot a snake in the grass quickly from the air, but you can do something about it much faster if you're on the ground.

⑧ Industrial espionage

If a snake can't catch a bird, it might try to steal an egg. In the same way, if a country doesn't have its own jet aircraft or computer technology, it might try to steal secrets to learn how to make its own. Many countries have moved the focus of their attacks away from military targets to financial and commercial ones, and it is estimated that there are currently 100 countries engaged in economic espionage.

It's all political

When Russia had a political row with its neighbor Estonia in 2007, Russian cyber spies crippled computer networks in Estonia for nearly two weeks. Russia was accused of doing the same thing to Georgia prior to the Ossetian, or Russia–Georgia, war in 2008.

Jet-setters

Between 2007 and 2009, Chinese spies allegedly broke into the computer networks of American technology company Lockheed Martin. The spies stole thousands of gigabytes of top secret details about a new fighter jet called the Joint Strike Fighter, which was being designed for the United States and British militaries.

Ghost in the machine

In 2009, a Chinese cyber-espionage network, code-named "GhostNet," was accused of infecting computers all over the world with a virus so that it could access them. GhostNet could search an infected computer's hard drive, tap into e-mails, and even use the machine's webcam and microphone to record conversations.

Who are the cyber spies?

Thanks to the World Wide Web, a cyber spy could be accessing your computer from anywhere in the world. All kinds of people dabble in cyber espionage and it's not just criminals. Big companies and marketing firms track your buying habits and movements on the Internet, companies snoop on rival businesses' networks to steal their ideas, and even government agents use the Web to keep an eye on what other countries are up to.

CYBER SPIES

Today, we are totally reliant upon computers and the Internet. They run our jobs, our social lives, our transportation networks, our national security, and our power grids. But what if someone were to use this technology against us to steal our secrets, or our identities? Welcome to the world of the cyber spy.

Google

Open sesame

In 2010, cyber spies from China stole one of Google's source codes, which gave them access to Google's global password system. Once they had these details, they could hack into the e-mail accounts of Gmail users around the world.

Nuclear meltdown

In 2010, a piece of malicious computer software called the "Stuxnet worm" attacked computer systems in five of Iran's nuclear enrichment plants. Stuxnet targeted command and control systems that caused machinery in the plants to fail, and is one of the most advanced pieces of malware ever discovered.

Power to the people

In 2010, it was reported that spies from China and Russia had hacked into the control systems of the U.S. electricity grid. No harm was done but it exposed a vulnerability: If the grid had been shut down, millions of people would have been left without electricity.

Unexpected homework

In 2010, a high school in Philadelphia issued their students laptop PCs to do their homework on. The school had installed spyware on the computers so they could find them if they went missing. The plan backfired, however, when the school was accused of using the hidden cameras to spy on their students at home.

Watch out!

The Internet is the cyber spy's "back door" to your computer. Malicious software that collects your data or disrupts your computer can be hidden in seemingly innocent e-mails or websites. E-mails that link to fake banking websites can also trick you into giving away private information.

SPY WORLD

Threats to national security come in many different guises. It might be an improvised bomb from a terrorist group, or a weapon of mass destruction from a secretive nation. Traditional spying techniques may not be able to gather the information that's needed, so intelligence agencies have learned to use less direct methods, one of which is Measurement and Signature Intelligence (MASINT), to find out what enemies are up to...

Shaky ground

Seismic detectors trace vibrations as they travel underground. Used to measure earthquakes, they also have a place in the spy lab for monitoring enemy nuclear weapons programs. Should the enemy happen to test a bomb, seismic detectors can identify the kind of bomb and where it exploded.

Into the darkness

Finding anything in the hustle and bustle of a city is a difficult job. Buildings get in the way and the streets are often dirty or smoggy. Lasers can pierce the gloom and make highly accurate maps of the environment. You can also analyze the laser light that bounces back for suspicious chemical evidence.

Dirty dealings

If a hostile country is building a nuclear device, you'll want to know about it. Fortunately, the nuclear materials used to build weapons are dirty and require lots of processing. By monitoring suspect areas for unusual levels of radiation, you can identify where a device is being built.

Chemical tasting

What if a country has developed weapons of mass destruction but official inspectors have found nothing? One way to identify any weapon-testing is to "taste" for the chemical signature that it would leave behind. If a missile was tested, it would leave a chemical trail in the atmosphere as it burned fuel.

Watery waves

An enemy might think that they can sneak around unmonitored at sea. But they aren't counting on the sonar warning system. Sound waves from a ship's engine travel a long way underwater, and a network of ocean-based microphones can identify an enemy ship from its acoustic signature.

Say cheese!

Satellites provide sneaky ways to photograph suspicious areas, but what if all they show are harmless trees and fields? Infrared cameras can detect the heat signatures of people and machinery that might be camouflaged from view, while ultraviolet images reveal any chemicals that wouldn't be in an "innocent" field.

FIGHTING TERROR

Terrorists don't play by the rules. They have no regard for the law, they are very difficult to track down, and they are highly unpredictable. This makes anticipating and preventing an attack very difficult. Counterterrorism requires the use of many tools and many different tactics. Some are subtle, some are aggressive, and some are controversial, but they are all needed in the fight against terror.

Intelligence

The collection and analysis of intelligence is the first line of defense, but it does have its limitations. Infiltrating a group of terrorists who are suspicious of outsiders is almost impossible, so any intelligence gathered is likely to be fragmentary, vague, and possibly unreliable. This makes the job of the analyst very challenging and can provide only a rough picture of which terrorists pose a threat where, and how they might attack. Even knowing all these things can't guarantee that an attack will be prevented.

Diplomacy

A job is often easier with the help of friends. Terrorist networks such as al-Qaeda operate across multiple countries, so it's important that those countries are willing to cooperate against the terrorists. Diplomacy is a powerful tool that encourages cooperation and brings countries together. After the September 11 attacks, the United Nations Security Council passed a law that outlawed terrorism and financing it, restricted the movements of terrorist organizations, and forced countries to disclose information about terrorists. Unfortunately, it failed to define what a terrorist is.

Law enforcement

While the law is unlikely to act as a deterrent to a terrorist, it can be useful in preventing an attack if a terrorist is caught. Criminal law has been a powerful tool in the fight against terrorism, but it also raises the problem of human rights. In 2003, Malaysia was criticized by human rights groups for passing counterterrorism laws that limited their citizens' movements and freedom of speech. By imprisoning suspected terrorists without a proper trial, many other countries also face allegations of human rights violations.

Financial controls

For a business to operate successfully, it needs money, and terrorism is no different. Governments can try to cut off funding by freezing the assets of individuals, but the money will often pass through middlemen and money launderers, making it difficult to figure out which individuals the money is coming from. Also, many materials that terrorists need, such as explosives, can be purchased relatively cheaply, and such small dealings are difficult to trace. The Madrid train bombings in 2004, for example, required only a few thousand dollars' worth of explosives.

Military force

Terrorist organizations are often small groups that don't make easy targets for military strikes. Many countries have Special Forces units—elite tactical groups that are trained to directly engage terrorists and prevent attacks. Some countries, such as Israel, have been using Special Forces teams in counterterrorist actions for decades. A Palestinian terrorist group called the PLO hijacked 82 planes during 1969 alone. When they hijacked Air France flight 139 in 1974, Israeli Special Forces stormed the airport terminal in Uganda and rescued 102 hostages.

Soft power

Anger is the fuel of terrorism. Terrorist recruiters exploit people's anger to motivate members of a community to support them. Soft-power counterterrorism tactics use the media to spread messages that help defuse some of that anger. It is the subtlest of the counterterrorism tools, but it can be highly effective. One of the countries leading the way in the use of this tactic is Saudi Arabia. This Muslim country was vulnerable to terrorist messages, but the government has counteracted them through education, as well as television, newspaper, and Internet campaigns.

MISSION: BIOLOGY

In the past, all a spy needed to sneak past security was a counterfeit passport, a fake mustache, and a fishy foreign accent. But these days, they have their work cut out for them. Modern biometric systems use scanners, cameras, and vast computer databases of personal records to identify a person based on an array of physical characteristics that are almost impossible to disguise.

FACE UP TO IT

Your face is unique—no one else has one quite like it. Digital facial recognition systems can identify you from a photo or video frame by measuring your facial proportions and matching them up with a database. So big-nosed spies need not apply.

TOOTH OR DARE

Dental recognition takes advantage of how everyone's teeth grow and wear down differently. Usually, this X-ray technique is reserved for dead people who are unrecognizable due to, say, being flattened by a rhino, but it may also be used to get you before the rhino does.

SPEAK AND YE SHALL FIND

Even if you can't see a person's face, you might recognize them from their voice. Computers can use voice verification software to measure the different tone, pitch, and rhythm of a person's voice to make an audio fingerprint (voiceprint), which can be matched to a database.

THE EYES HAVE IT

Your iris (the colored ring around your pupil) is made up of a complex pattern of ridges and colors, unique to you. Iris scanners can map all those ridges for storage in a database and identify you faster than you can blink.

EARS LOOKING AT YOU

Did you know that your ear's structure is as individual as a fingerprint? No? Well, scientists do, and have developed a system that uses reflected light to map all the tubes and lobes that make your ear special. The system is eerily accurate.

178

PRINT AMONG THIEVES

No two fingerprints are alike—the pattern of loops and swirls is unique to its owner. Used as a method of identification for more than 600 years, fingerprints can be scanned electronically these days and used to secure doors and access computers, as well as to catch the odd criminal or two.

WALK THIS WAY

Each of us moves, walks, and runs in ways that are subtly different from others. Gait analysis systems use cameras and special software to identify individuals from their movements. They can also reveal if a person is hiding something that affects how they walk (such as a heavy weapon).

YOU'RE SO VEIN

The palm of your hand hides a network of veins in a treelike pattern that is totally unique. Handily, all that warm blood they carry shows up brightly on infrared scanners, and can be compared with a database to identify you.

SIGN LANGUAGE

Everyone has a different way of writing: of slanting, curling, and forming their letters, words, and sentences. This makes writing very difficult to disguise or duplicate. Handwriting experts can quickly tell if a signature has been forged, and some people think handwriting can reveal facts about your personality.

DNA

The set of chemical instructions that makes you you, telling your cells how to behave and grow, is called DNA (deoxyribonucleic acid). Unless you are a twin, your DNA is unique to you and is the ultimate fingerprint. It can be extracted from any part of you and broken down to create a sort of genetic bar code.

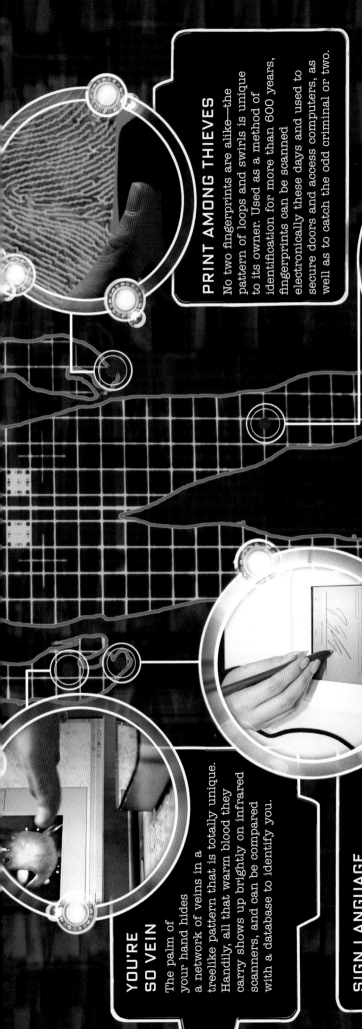

GO!

You step outside

Whoops, you walked right into that one! Within minutes of stepping outside, you're caught on closed-circuit television (CCTV). In cities especially, cameras monitor streets, stores, public transportation, cash machines, and—if you walk past one—you, too! Foiled at the first roll, you should just start again. Go back a space!

GO BACK A SPACE

HOME!

You're home

Phew! You made it home and are safe now, right? Wrong. Online marketing companies can track your Internet preferences and then send you information on products based on your web searches. And that fancy new television can keep tabs on what shows you watch—it helps you not miss an episode, but also adds to the database of information about you. You relaxed too quickly. Go back a space!

THE GAME OF SURVEILLANCE

You might be minding your own business, but right from the word "go," someone or something is monitoring your activities every day. Our modern world is one big spy state, where almost every move you make leaves an electronic footprint that can be traced, logged, and exploited by companies, governments, and even criminals. Can you make it home without being spied on? Roll the dice to see how far you get...

MISS A TURN

You slip on a banana peel

Your throbbing ankle needs some attention, but be careful what information you divulge to your doctor. Your personal records, medical details, and possibly your DNA profile are all gathered and stored in a central database. In 2010, one of these servers in Dublin, Ireland, was hacked and a million records were stolen. You hobble home, slowly. Miss a turn!

GO FORWARD A SPACE

There's no traffic

You hit the accelerator thinking you can zoom past without anyone noticing and make up for lost time. Bad move—cameras that can identify and record license plates are used at speed checkpoints, traffic lights, and even on the backs of buses! You lose your licence for speeding. Miss a turn!

You catch the train

You hope to hide among the crowds on the subway but there's no hiding here either. Many city networks operate using electronic tickets that are registered with the user's name and address. Every time the ticket is swiped at a turnstyle, a magnetic reader logs the ticket's—and person's—location. The data can be used to track travel patterns. You opt for a single paper ticket. Very clever—go forward a space!

GO FORWARD A SPACE

You get to school

To enter the doors, you must swipe your electronic ID. Some schools, and most companies, issue electronic ID cards to swipe in and out of building security systems. They record your time of arrival and movements within the site. You're caught sleeping in and arriving late. You have to stay after hours to make up the lost time. Go back a space!

Who was the original Tonton Macoute?

In Haiti, during the 1950s and 1960s, the Haitian secret police, the MVSN, made citizens who disagreed with the government's policies disappear. Locals called the abductors the "Tonton Macoute" after a mythical Haitian bogeyman who stole children by stuffing them into sacks.

Who were the Mississippi spies spying on?

Also during the 1950s and 1960s, the U.S. civil rights movement was fighting to end the segregation of African-Americans and give them the vote. The Mississippi government didn't want this to happen, so they set up a network of informants that infiltrated civil rights organizations and tried to undermine their activities.

How much do you know about spy states in history? Pick a card for a chance to roll again.

GO BACK A SPACE

You go shopping

You pop out to go shopping but unwittingly give away all kinds of personal details. Every time you withdraw cash from an ATM or use a credit card, your location is logged by the bank. Stores will also try to sign you up for their loyalty cards, but beware—these make a record of everything that you buy. You decline their offer. Go forward a space!

ROLL AGAIN

You make a call

Even if you're not actually using your phone, it will still emit a signal to nearby phone towers, pinpointing your exact location. The police can request this information from telecommunications companies when they are looking for someone. Luckily, you're not a criminal so no one cares what you're saying. Roll again!

THE MAN WHO TRIED TO DISAPPEAR

THE NAME'S BOND, DAVID BOND!

I AM NOT A SPY, BUT I AM ON THE RUN, AND BEING HUNTED...

IT ALL STARTED A FEW MONTHS AGO. I RECEIVED A LETTER FROM THE UK'S CHILD BENEFIT OFFICE INFORMING ME THAT MY DAUGHTER'S RECORDS HAD BEEN LOST. ALONG WITH 25 MILLION OTHER PEOPLE, I LEARNED THAT PRIVATE DATA, INCLUDING MY BANK DETAILS, HAD GONE MISSING.

EVERY ADULT IN THE UK IS REGISTERED ON MORE THAN 700 DATABASES AND IS CAUGHT SEVERAL TIMES A DAY ON THE FIVE MILLION CCTV CAMERAS THAT COVER THE UK IN A SURVEILLANCE GRID.

I WANTED TO KNOW HOW MUCH MORE OF MY PERSONAL INFORMATION WAS BEING STORED OUT THERE. I WROTE TO 80 GOVERNMENT AND COMMERCIAL ORGANIZATIONS, ASKING THEM TO HAND OVER WHATEVER THEY HAD ON ME.

I WAS SHOCKED. THEY KNEW WHAT WEBSITES I VISITED, WHO MY FRIENDS WERE, AND EVEN WHERE I'D DRIVEN MY CAR. ONE COMPANY EVEN NOTED THAT I HAD "SOUNDED ANGRY" ON A PHONE CALL TO MY BANK IN 2006.

THIS FREAKED ME OUT SO MUCH THAT I DECIDED TO GO OFF THE GRID AND DISAPPEAR ALTOGETHER. I PACKED MY BAGS, SAID GOODBYE TO MY PREGNANT WIFE, AND TRIED TO VANISH. IMMEDIATELY, I BECAME A HUNTED MAN.

WITHIN HOURS, A GROUP OF INVESTIGATORS CALLED CERBERUS HAD PLANTED A TRACKING DEVICE ON MY WIFE'S CAR. THEY FOUND OUT SHE WAS PREGNANT AND CALLED THE HOSPITAL, PRETENDING TO BE ME, TO FIND OUT OUR APPOINTMENTS.

HELLO, THIS IS DAVID BOND. CAN YOU TELL ME IF WE HAVE AN APPOINTMENT THIS WEEK?

LET ME CHECK FOR YOU, MR. BOND.

BY THIS POINT, I HAD ALREADY LEFT THE COUNTRY AND WAS ON A EUROSTAR TRAIN TO BELGIUM. THE INVESTIGATORS HAD ANTICIPATED THIS, THOUGH. PRETENDING TO BE ME, THEY HAD CALLED THE FERRY OPERATOR, TRAIN COMPANIES, AND AIRLINES TO SEE IF MY CREDIT CARD HAD BEEN USED.

IS THAT ONE OF THEM? SURELY NOT... THEY COULDN'T FIND ME SO FAST.

LUCKILY, I HAD USED A FRIEND'S CREDIT CARD AND A FALSE NAME, SO I WAS SAFE—BUT NOT FOR LONG. SHORTLY AFTER ARRIVING IN BELGIUM, A VIDEO OF ME WAS POSTED ONLINE. THEY KNEW WHERE I WAS! BUT I WAS ONE STEP AHEAD, AND ON MY WAY TO GERMANY.

THAT'S HIM!

YEP, HE'S IN BELGIUM.

MEANWHILE... CERBERUS USED THE INTERNET TO HUNT ME DOWN. I HAD CLOSED MY SOCIAL-NETWORKING PROFILES BUT CERBERUS RETRIEVED THEM AND USED THE INFORMATION TO SET UP A FALSE PAGE. USING THE NAME PHILEAS FOGG, THEY PRETENDED TO BE ME.

THEY CONTACTED MY FRIENDS AND SAID THAT THIS WAS MY SECRET PROFILE PAGE AND THAT THEY SHOULD GET IN TOUCH. LOTS OF MY FRIENDS DID, MEANING MY PURSUERS WERE ABLE TO CRASH ANY PARTIES THEY HELD TO TRY AND GET INFORMATION FROM THEM.

SO HOW DO YOU KNOW DAVID?

OH, WE GO WAAAY BACK... SO WHAT'S HE UP TO THESE DAYS?

THEY EVEN WENT THROUGH MY TRASH FOR OLD RECEIPTS, BILLS, AND LETTERS TO SEE IF THERE WERE ANY CLUES TO WHERE I WAS GOING.

IN THE MEANTIME, I HAD MADE IT TO GERMANY. I MADE SURE TO PAY FOR EVERYTHING IN CASH, WHICH I WITHDREW FROM CASH MACHINES AT THE LAST POSSIBLE MOMENT SO I COULD GET A HEAD START BEFORE THE TRANSACTIONS WERE TRACED, BUT THE DETECTIVES TRACKED DOWN THE WITHDRAWALS AND WERE HOT ON MY TRAIL.

THE TRAIN FOR BERLIN IS ABOUT TO DEPART FROM PLATFORM TWO.

THEY SENT MESSAGES TO MY PHONE HOPING THAT I WOULD REPLY AND GIVE MYSELF AWAY, BUT I WAS ON THE MOVE AGAIN.

We know you've been to Belgium and Germany

I HAD DECIDED TO GO BACK TO ENGLAND BUT I HAD A BAD FEELING ABOUT MY EUROSTAR TICKET, SO AT THE LAST MINUTE I DECIDED TO TAKE THE FERRY. LUCKY I DID... CERBERUS WAS WAITING FOR ME AT THE EUROSTAR TERMINAL AT ST. PANCRAS STATION IN LONDON.

HE'S NOT HERE!

I STAYED AT MY DAD'S HOUSE IN KENT, JUST OUTSIDE LONDON, FOR A NIGHT. PARANOIA WAS REALLY SETTING IN. I WAS CONVINCED THAT A BUGGING DEVICE HAD BEEN HIDDEN IN MY BAGS SO I TORE EVERYTHING APART. THERE WAS NOTHING THERE.

THE NEXT MORNING, THERE WAS A KNOCK AT THE DOOR... WAS IT THEM? HAD THEY FOUND ME? I HAD TO GET OUT OF THERE! MY FATHER DISTRACTED THEM WHILE I SNUCK OUT THE WINDOW. THAT WAS TOO CLOSE! I HAD TO FIND A BETTER PLACE TO HIDE.

HOLD ON, I'M COMING! UMM, WHO IS IT?

I BORROWED A CAR FROM A FRIEND AND DROVE TO WALES WHERE I HID IN A WOODEN SHACK IN THE WOODS. BUT CONSTANTLY WORRYING ABOUT GETTING CAUGHT WAS TAKING ITS TOLL. I COULDN'T SLEEP AND MY IMAGINATION WAS REALLY RUNNING RIOT.

OH GOD, THEY'RE HERE...

THEY'VE FOUND ME!

THEY HADN'T FOUND ME, BUT THE NEXT DAY I RECEIVED A CALL FROM MY WIFE ON A PREPAID PHONE I'D BOUGHT BEFORE I LEFT IN CASE OF EMERGENCIES.

I HAVE TO GO TO THE HOSPITAL.

I'LL BE THERE AS SOON AS I CAN.

I TRAVELED BACK TO LONDON AND CHECKED INTO A CHEAP HOTEL. WHEN I WENT TO THE HOSPITAL, MY WIFE WAS FINE BUT THERE WAS SOMETHING ODD ABOUT SOME OF THE PEOPLE IN THE WAITING ROOM...

THAT'S ODD, SHE DOESN'T LOOK VERY PREGNANT...

IT WAS CERBERUS! THEY HAD DISCOVERED THAT MY WIFE HAD AN APPOINTMENT AND THEY WERE WAITING FOR ME. AFTER JUST 18 DAYS ON THE RUN, I HAD BEEN CAUGHT!

BUT THERE WAS NO BULLET TO THE HEAD! THEY WEREN'T HERE TO KILL ME. I AM A FILMMAKER, AND I HAD ACTUALLY HIRED CERBERUS MYSELF TO TRY AND TRACK ME DOWN. IT WAS AN EXPERIMENT TO SEE IF, IN TODAY'S SURVEILLANCE SOCIETY, IT'S POSSIBLE TO GO OFF THE GRID AND ESCAPE... IT ISN'T.

LATER, THEY SHOWED ME THEIR OFFICE WHERE THEY HAD EVERYTHING ABOUT ME PINNED UP ON A WALL. THEY CALLED IT MY "DATA WAKE." ALL THEY HAD AT FIRST WAS MY NAME AND MY PHOTO, AND NOW HERE THEY WERE WITH MY ENTIRE LIFE SPREAD ACROSS A WALL.

THE MAN WHO TRIED TO DISAPPEAR 183

WHAT DOES THE FUTURE HOLD?

The changing threats and new technologies of recent decades have meant that the art of spying has had to change faster than ever before. New gadgetry, such as biometrics, has made a spy's job both easier and more difficult, while robot spies could soon be stepping from the pages of science fiction into reality.

Predicting the future

Many governments employ special groups, such as the National Intelligence Council (NIC) in the United States, whose job is to predict the future. In place of crystal balls and sacrificial goats, current trends are analyzed in a much more scientific way to forecast where threats and conflicts might come from in the future. The findings are then reported to policy makers.

Cyborg spies

A cyborg is a biological organism that has been enhanced with mechanical or electrical components. Imagine a spy who can upload thoughts to a computer—what spooky reading that would make—or even one with a bionic eye that can zoom in on distant objects and see in the dark! It might sound far-fetched, but eye implants that allow blind people to see basic images already exist.

Robot spies

Cyborg insects are all well and good, but all it takes is one well-timed swat for Beetle Bond to meet a sticky end, so the future of miniature spying could be full-on robotics. Engineers are taking cues from nature and creating tiny, fully robotic insects that are armed with mini cameras and microphones. Some of these robo-bugs resemble flies, but there are also robotic spiders and jellylike caterpillars that can squeeze through cracks and under doors!

Cyborg insects

It might be a while before cyborg human spies go into the field, but cyborg insect spies are almost a reality. These sneaky crawlies had tiny cameras and control devices implanted into their bodies when they were still larvae. As they grew, the miniature mechanisms became part of their bodies, allowing them to be used as remote-controlled spies.

K-G-BEE

F-BEE-I

Don't write off the human

Although computers are becoming increasingly sophisticated, they still can't replace a human's ability to solve problems, make deductions, and adapt to complex situations. A human spy can blend in, persuade, and coerce. A robot can't. Robots can't use subtle reasoning to persuade a rival spy to switch sides, nor can they seduce an enemy's secretary into handing over top secret intelligence. Humans will always be the key spies in the complex world of espionage.

Cyber warfare

What would happen if an enemy took control of a country's power grid or defense systems? Most countries agree that cyber attacks will be one of the biggest threats to their national security in the future. Countries that used to be rivals are now working together to establish international laws and strategies to prevent cyber threats.

Wikileaks

The world of espionage has always been about trying to uncover and protect secrets. Organizations such as Wikileaks are making the former easier and the latter much more difficult by providing the means through which individuals can release top secret information into the public domain. In theory, this means that governments and the intelligence community will be more accountable for their actions, since all it takes is one person clicking a button for the lowdown on secret missions to be made available to the world.

Communications

How will spies communicate with each other in the future? Cyborg spies might have it covered with brain-to-brain e-mails, but what about the all-human spies? In 2006, the U.S. intelligence community created "Intellipedia" to fix communication problems between the different security agencies. It allows analysts to add, edit, and share intelligence with agencies across the United States.

Spy speak

SPY OPERATIONS

Black bag job
Secret entry into a home or office to steal or copy materials, or to install a bug

Black operations
Covert activities

Brush pass
A brief encounter where something is passed between two agents

Data haunts
Collecting electronic information about someone without leaving a trace

Dry cleaning
Actions agents take to ensure that they are not under surveillance

Exfiltration operation
A secret rescue operation designed to bring an agent or other person out of harm's way

False flag
An operation in which the recruiting officer approaches a target under the guise of representing the intelligence agency of another country

Flaps and seals
Opening, examining, and resealing envelopes and packages without raising suspicion

Pretexting
Obtaining information by pretending to be someone else

Sanitizing
Deleting specific material or revising a report or document to prevent the identification of intelligence sources and collection methods, usually done in the process of "declassification" (release to the public) of information

Sweep
To check a room for bugs

Takedown
The destruction of a network of enemy agents

Wet job
An operation in which blood is shed; a KGB term for an assassination

AGENTS

Bagman
An agent who carries or delivers money

Bird-watcher
Slang used by British intelligence for a spy

Case officer
An intelligence officer who controls an agent; the CIA term for an agent handler

Developmental
A potential agent courted by a case officer

Mole
An agent of one organization who has penetrated a specific organization or intelligence agency by gaining employment

Raven
A male agent employed to seduce people for intelligence purposes. A female is called a swallow. Both terms were used principally by the KGB and East German intelligence.

Sleeper
Agent living as an ordinary citizen in a foreign country; acts only when directed by his or her controlling intelligence agency

Spook
Slang term for an operative

Walk-in
An agent who offers their services and may or may not be recruited

USEFUL PEOPLE

Babysitter
Bodyguard

Cleaner
A person who removes incriminating evidence at the scene of a crime

Cobbler or shoemaker
A person who creates false passports, visas, diplomas, and other documents

Cutout
A middleman (or woman) who wittingly or unwittingly provides a degree of separation between two others—for example, between the head of a spy ring and its members

Floater
A person used one time, occasionally, or even unknowingly for an intelligence operation

Nursemaid
The security officer who accompanies Russian delegations to other countries to prevent anyone from defecting

White coats
Doctors

INFORMATION

Chicken feed
Convincing, but not critical, intelligence knowingly provided to an enemy intelligence agency through an agent or a double agent working for an opposing organization

Ears only
Material too sensitive to commit to writing

Eyes only
Documents that may be read but not discussed; documents intended only "for the eyes of" (i.e., to be read by) a specific person or persons

Handle
Information or other means by which a case officer exerts control over an agent

The take
Information gathered by espionage

SPY GEAR

Funny money
Counterfeit banknotes

L-pill
A poison pill used to commit suicide—"L" stands for *lethal*

Pocket litter
Items in a spy's pocket (coins, tickets, receipts) that add authenticity to his or her identity

Shoe
False passport or visa

TAKING SIDES

Allies
The countries that fought against the Axis powers in World War II. The Allies included the United States, Britain, and the Soviet Union.

Axis
The countries that fought against the Allies in World War II. Germany, Japan, and Italy were the leading Axis countries.

OSS
Office of Strategic Services. This was a World War II American intelligence agency. After the war, parts of it were incorporated into the new CIA (Central Intelligence Agency) in 1947.

SOE
Special Operations Executive. A British intelligence agency established during World War II— according to Prime Minister Winston Churchill, in order to "set Europe ablaze!"

United Nations
An organization established in 1945, at the end of World War II, to "unite all nations."

United Nations Security Council
Consisting of 15 member countries, the Security Council's role is to try and maintain international peace and security.

USSR
Union of Soviet Socialist Republics. This is the full name for the Soviet Union, the Communist state that incorporated Russia and many surrounding countries. It was established in 1922 and broke up in 1991.

CONFLICTS

American Revolution
During the American Revolution, the original 13 U.S. colonies rejected the authority of Britain, the colonial power that governed them. In 1775, they went to war with Britain to win their independence. The conflict lasted until 1783.

Civil War
A war between the states of the United States, 1861–1865. The war began when 11 Southern states broke away from the Union to form a government of their own—the Confederacy. The Union fought back to prevent the break up of the nation.

Cold War
A period of tension between two world superpowers—the United States and the Soviet Union—and their allies. Each side suspected the other, and developed nuclear weapons. Began at the end of World War II and lasted until the Soviet Union broke up in 1991.

World War I
Sometimes referred to as the Great War, this conflict lasted from 1914 to 1918. Most world nations joined one of the two opposing sides—the Central Powers (led by Germany, Austria-Hungary, and the Ottoman Empire) and the Allies (led by Britain, France, Belgium, Italy, and Russia). During the war, more than 20 million people were killed.

World War II
A global conflict, 1939–1945. The two opposing sides were the Allies and the Axis countries. War first broke out in Europe. Britain and France went to war with Nazi Germany, which later invaded the Soviet Union. The United States entered the war in 1941, when Japanese planes bombed the U.S. fleet in Pearl Harbor, Hawaii. The war killed 55 million people.

Index

T

UV

Acknowledgments

DK WOULD LIKE TO THANK:
Peter Earnest, Jacqueline Eyl, Amanda Ohlke, Anna Slafer, and Mark Stout of the International Spy Museum for their expertise and insight into the spy world.

Hannah Bagshaw, David M Buisan, Seb Burnett, Rich Cando, Stephen Chan, Karen Cheung, Jim Cohen, Fay Dalton, Allan Deas, Camellie Dobrin, Hunt Emerson, Mike Hall, Infomen, Matt Johnstone, Jan Kallwejt, Toby Leigh, Ellen Lindner, Mark Longworth, Joel Millerchip, Ralph Pitchford, Keiran Sandal, Serge Seidlitz, Mike Stones, and Lucas Varela for illustrations.

Sarah Owens for proofreading and Jackie Brind for the index. Harriet Mills, Ria Jones, Rob Nunn, Sarah Smithies, Karen VanRoss, and Jo Walton for picture research.

PICTURE CREDITS
The publisher would like to thank the following for their kind permission to reproduce their photographs:
(Key: a-above; b-below/bottom; c-center; f-far; l-left; r-right; t-top)

akg-images: North Wind Picture Archives 40bl, 149tr, 149ftl, 152tc; **Alamy Images:** The Art Archive 134cla, Howard Barlow 117c (8), James Boardman 6tl, 13bc, 97r, Crash Media Group 23bl, Olaf Doering 94cl (4 bottles), Michael Gilday 161fclb, Nic Hamilton 115cla, Chris Howes / Wild Places Photography 153b (barbed wire), Ken Hugill 167crb (poster (merged)), INTERFOTO 115br (bird), 116 (1), 153bc, 41cr, 43br, 115tc, 117 (6), 160cr, 161cra, ITAR-TASS Photo Agency 167crb (Gorbachev), Lebrecht Music and Arts Photo Library 143bl, Manor Photography 86-87, North Wind Picture Archives 153tl, Oramstock 153c, Ron Chapple Stock 116-117 (feet), Maurice Savage 167cr, Alex Segre 152-153 (background), SUNNYphotography.com 94-95 (background), Trinity Mirror / Mirrorpix 67tl, Yagil Henkin 80-81 (background), Ron Yue 176-177 (faces); **© Courtesy John Alexander / www.enigmaandfriends.com:** 83cla, 83clb; **The Art Archive:** Musée du Louvre Paris 133cr; **The Bridgeman Art Library:** Ashmolean Museum, University of Oxford, UK 132ca, Giraudon 149bl; **Richard Brisson, Ottawa Canada – www.campx.ca:** 82br; **William L. Clements Library, The University Of Michigan:** 90crb; **Collection of the Litchfield Historical Society, Litchfield, Connecticut:** 42tl; **Corbis:** Yusuke Nakanishi / Aflo 6tr, 119r, Jeff Albertson 153bl (trapdoor), David Arky 36ftl, Nathan Benn 176-177 (main image), Bettmann 42cl (No.1), 43tr, 43bl (No.2), 49tc, 115cl, 156cl, 156c, 158fcra, 166c, Bill Perry / Bettmann 43bl (No.4), Vince Mannino / Bettmann 43bl (No.3), Bloomimage 172tc, Matthew Borkoski / Monsoon / Photolibrary 172fcr, Canopy 23br (syringe), Alison Clarke 65cla (tree), Frank Conlon / Star Ledger 104-105, Digital Art 114tl, Peter Oetzmann / epa 176-177 (fire), Randy Faris 173cb (laptop), Wolfgang Flamisch 36-37 (plans), Kai Foersterling / epa 173tc, Martyn Goddard 115bl, Nathan Griffith 64-65 (park), Tom Grill 172clb (globe), Hulton-Deutsch Collection 42cl (No.2), Roy Scott / Images.com 173tr, Images.com 173cb (screen), Helen King 20cr, Natalia Kolesnikova/ POOL / epa 67c, Antonin Kratochvil / VII 7tl, 147r, Charles & Josette Lenars 132br, Barry Lewis / In Pictures 124tr (gun barrel), 124tr (gun repeats), Melvyn Longhurst 37br, Charlie Mahoney 142cr, Lawrence Manning 23cr, Mika 65bc, Ocean 173c, Michael Prince 22cl, Redlink 159t, Benjamin Rondel 65ca, David Selman 152fbr, Shepard Sherbell / Corbis SABA 167crb (poster), Sygma 67ftl, Leszek Szymanski 167tc, Paul Thompson / National Geographic Society 156-157 (main image), TongRo Image Stock / 173cr (camera), Varie / Alt 70cb, Victor Habbick Visions / Science Photo Library 172tr, Josh Westrich 172tl, David Jordan Williams 172fcl, Tim Wright 43bl (No.1); **Courtesy Corner Shot (Israel) Ltd.:** 117 (9); **Courtesy Pustak Mahal, New Delhi:** 121tr; **Alastair H Cummings/University of Southampton:** 178crb; **Dorling Kindersley:** Geoff Brightling / Denoyer-Geppert - modelmaker © Denoyer-Geppert 143br, Tina Chambers © National Maritime Museum, London 82bl, Chas Howson © The British Museum 149cr (coins), Geoff Dann / National Museums of Scotland 138br (medal), Gary Ombler © Dorling Kindersley, Courtesy of Tablehurst Farm 125ca (sausages), Gary Ombler / Courtesy of the Board of Trustees of the Royal Armouries 124crb (gun), Gary Ombler © Dorling Kindersley, Courtesy of Richard Simms 161cla, James Stevenson © Dorling Kindersley, Courtesy of the National Maritime Museum, London 124tl; **Dreamstime.com:** 5xinc 201 (blue bin), Abdulsatarid 171fcr, Acedubai 132c (barrel), Algol 131bc, Alhovik 152crb, Andreasg 173br (screen), Andygaylor 23bc (camera), Anechka 91bl (plug), Baloncici 13bl, 41tl (oval frame), Beaniebeagle 87bc (book), Benglim 120-121 (metal spiral), Bharatpandey 87c (yellow), Bluemorpho 153fclb (bullets), Brookefuller 49bl, Cammeraydave 102cl, Claudiodivizia 13bc (CCTV), Clearviewstock 87fcr (gold), Coraldesign 125br, Cornishman 86r (enigma machine), Crisp 148br, davidundderriese 42-43 (background), Dbjohnston 95ca (bottles behind), Dcb 102clb, Demian1975 133cb, Dlvv 95ca (bottles front), Dragoneye 152cb (wagon), Pablo Eder 160cra (box), 160cb (wallet), Ekaterinasemenova 112-113, Ensiferrum 87tl (chess), Ermess 12cr (white poster), Fibobjects 23c (lifejacket), Fmatte 125br (tag), Fonzie26 132tr, Francy874 82 (border), Garry518 41cl (eye), Garygrc02 100-101 (background), Gemenacom 22-23 (hooks), Gigiodesign 106-107 (eye), Gl0ck33 124cl, Grynold 42-43 (handcuffs icon), Grzym 103clb (ace card), 103bl (10 spades), Haizul 177bc, Highlaz 12c, Hpphoto 40-41 (gold frames), Ijansempoi 48tc, Ika767 171cra, Isatori 40ftr, Jcjgphotography 125crb, Kaetana 20clb (papers), Kenny1 20-21b (background), Klodien 153crb, Kmitu 40bl (price tag), Korzeniewski 23cl, Krisdog 12fcrb, Kurkul 171crb, Lagui 21cr, Lordalea 171tc (virus), Loskutnikov 124bc (bow), 125ca, Luceluceluce 120 (background), Mailthepic 124cl (ribbon), Marilynv 95ca (bottle tags), Maximkostenko 40bl (sofa), Mer08 42-43 (handshake icon), 176bc, Miflippo 12cra (banner), 103cla, Mihail39 100-101 (bubbles), Mike55555 90cl, Mohol 94cl (labels), Monbibi 149 (tape), Mykira 71tl (money), Nicemonkey 49br, Nikoladesign 142-143 (open pages), Nikolais 115tr, Nuttakit 124-125 (wall), Okno 152fbl, Paha_l 142-143 (border), 180-181 (background), Passigatti 125cb (paper), Paulina94 131fbl, Pedro2009 132-133 (background), Photographer 124-125 (shelves and typewriter), Picsfive 21cl (glue1), 21cl (glue2), Picstudio 48br, Popovaphoto 13cr (signs), Putnik70 103clb, Ralukatudor 49cr (website), Rcmathiraj 36-37 (paper), Rimglow 152bc (barrel), Rtguest 170cra, Rtimages 124clb (tape), Selvamartist 180bl (eye icon), 181fcl, Siart 177br, Sielemann 167clb, Simonasp 171cl, Snehitdesign 40tl (bookshelf), Sorsillo 12tc (blind), 13cl (blind), 13br (blind), Spanishalex 135c (hand), Sswartz 133fcr, Standaart 40-41 (frames), Stanko07 12crb, Stevanovicigor 102cr, Stocksnapper 116-117 (foam), Stoyanh 170ca, Tadija 49cla, Talli 170cr, Tielemans 20cr (green vase), Tootles 23br, Trosamange 153cr, Victoriaivanova 124cr, Viktorus 171tc (laptop), Vilax 124fcla, Vitalik-sv 135clb (hand), Winterling 121 (background), Woodsy007 21cl (skip), Xfox01 102br (pegs), Yurafx 40-41 (gold wall); **Fotolia:** amfarr 130c, barneyboogles 130tl, Florette Benoit 131fcr, BrankaVV 22cr (notebook), Bryan Busovicki 143tl (flag), Coprid 23cr (bag), Marc Dietrich 95bc, dipego 176bl, Adrian Hillman 167bl, Jut 130bl, Kamaga 131tr, Zbigniew Kosmal 94c (pins), Vladimir Liverts 22bc (camcorder), Alexander Lukin 177bl, Manish 112233 (page number icons), Bram J. Meijer 102cra (box), Minerva Studio 152cl, Madeleine Openshaw 94c (candle), Patrikeevna 170-171 (flags), Perysty 130tc, photodes 94t, picsfive 23c, Eduardo Rivero 123tr, sad 142-143 (background), Alexey Stiop 12-13 (building), tuulijumala 130br; **Getty Images:** AFP 42cl (No.4), 134clb, 179bl, the Agency Collection 90-91 (main image), amana images 12tl, William Andrew 65fcl (man), Archive Photos 143tr, 153tr, Shanna Baker/Flickr 102bl, Luc Beziat 138br, Michael Blann 139crb (mouse), Michael Blann 115r (field), Paul Bradbury 135cl (eyes), Philippe de Champaigne/The Bridgeman Art Library 133fcr (portrait), The Bridgeman Art Library 40ca, The Bridgeman Art Library / Chinese School 120tr, 133tl, Jean-Yves Bruel 172-173 (screens), David Buffington 116l (2), Lauren Burke 117 (11), C Squared Studios 159fcrb, Cavan Images 114-115 (sky), Vittorio Zunino Celotto 13br, Andrea Chu 81bl, Comstock 158fcr, Jeffrey Coolidge 87cra (receipts pile), Datacraft 59cl (chair), Peter Dazeley 66-67 (background), De Agostini 124cb (photo), DEA / G. Dagli Orti 149cla, Digital Vision 123br, Nick Dolding 87cra (receipt), DreamPictures 49br (newsreader), 172c (woman), Flickr Select/Jon Cartwright 138cb (pigeon), Tim Foster 138br (blanket), Fuse 139crb (brown mouse), Sheri L Giblin 139clb (cat), Jeffrey Hamilton 125cra, Leslie Harris 36-37 (background), GK Hart / Vikki Hart 134tr, Tim Hawley 139c (fin), Hulton Archive 42tr, 66cr, 67bl, 67tc, 67bc (body), 152cr 134cb (hand), 135cla (arm), 135cra, 135crb, Image Source 139br (wheelchair), Imagezoo / Images.com 94tr, Jose Luis Pelaez Inc 80cra, Lake County Museum 94cr (postcard), Ghislain & Marie David de Lossy 138-139 (background), Iain Masterton 166-167 (wall), Scott Morgan 13c (man), 91 (shadow), Simone Mueller 138bl, Muntz 22 (lockers), 23 (lockers), Matti Niemi 42br, NY Daily News via Getty Images 67c (Hedy Lamarr), Max Oppenheim 13tr, Panoramic Images 37cr, PHOTO 24 102-103 (background), photos_alyson 71tr, PM Images 12ftr, 180fbr, Popperfoto 42cl (No.3), Mike Powell 4tr, 31c, Siede Preis 68ftl, Pressphotos / Stringer 103bc, Redferns 66bc, Nicholas Rigg 70fcl (hand), 71fcr, Rubberball / Mike Kemp 12br, 80br, S. Solum / PhotoLink 80cla (sign), Andy Sacks 71bl, Ryuichi Sato 5tl, 53cr, Gail Shumway 142fcla, Erik Simonsen 107fcl, SMC Images 179cr, Pete Starman 139cb (white mouse), Stockbyte 161ca161clb (grenade), Stocktrek Images 114cl, SuperStock 41tl, Stephen Swintek 148-149 (chest, spade, earth), Cultura / Bill Sykes 71crb, Steve Taylor 116-117, Time & Life Pictures 95tr, 135ca (doll), Transcendental Graphics / Contributor 66cra (body), 66cra (head), U.S. Air Force / Handout 114cr, UHB Trust 178tc, Untitled X-Ray / Nick Veasey 58-59 (main) 59br (purse), 59br (wallet), 59br (briefcase), 59br (handkerchief), Betsie Van der Meer 139clb, Vintage Images 138cb, Dennis Welsh 80c (Kindi), Konrad Wothe / Minden 139fcla, Mel Yates 81c; **Greg Goebel/www.vectorsite.net:** 114tr; **Courtesy of the International Spy Museum:** 81cl, 83tl, 102br (buttons), 116 (3), 117 (7); **Mary Evans Picture Library:** 40cr; Harriet Mills: 160-161 (car boot); **National Cryptologic Museum:** Courtesy of the National Security Agency 5tr, 79r, 83bl; **The National Archives:** 116 (4); **NHPA / Photoshot:** Bill Love 170-171 (snakes); **Penguin Books Ltd:** Animal Farm by George Orwell © Courtesy Penguin UK 166bc; **Photolibrary:** Cocoon Cocoon 4tl, 11cr, Creativ Studio Heinemann 96-97, Datacraft 146-147, Flight Images LLP 174-175, Hartmut Schmidt / Imagebroker 118-119, Ingram Publishing RF 30-31, 52-53, 168-169, MIXA Co. Ltd. 81br (string phone), Photoalto 10-11, 78-79, Michael Prince 22-23 (bench), 22-23b, Red Cover 53br, Stockbroker 153fbr; **Press Association Images:** AP 90ca, 90cra, Franco Castano / AP 116br (5), Mikhail Metzel / AP 37tr, Lennart Preiss / AP 36cl; **Reuters:** Str Old 134br; **Paul Reuvers / Crypto Museum:** 83tr; **Rex Features:** Greg Mathieson 36bl; **Courtesy Lee Richards, www.psywar.org:** 160c (2); **The Royal Navy Submarine Museum:** 103c; **Science Museum / Science & Society Picture Library:** 83br (Colossus); **Science Photo Library:** Christian Darkin 82cr, 142bl, Coneyl Jay 178tl, James King-Holmes 179tl, Mehau Kulyk 178cra, PASIEKA 7tr, 169r, 178bc, 179tc; **Courtesy SOFTPRO GmbH / www.signplus.com:** 179cb; **TopFoto.co.uk:** 167cl, The Granger Collection 40tr, 41tc, 135fcla, 135fcl (hand), The National Archives / Heritage-Images 94br (music), RIA Novosti 135crb (hand), Topham Picturepoint 41c, 90cr, 91tl, UPP 83br (inset); **US Department of Defense:** www.defenseimagery.mil / TSGT Frank Garzelnick 114bc; **Werner Forman Archive:** National Museum, Beirut, Lebanon 149br; **Williamson-Dickie Europe Limited / www.dickiesworkwear.com:** 22cr

JACKET CREDITS
FRONT: istockphoto.com: Giovanni Banfi cla

All other images © Dorling Kindersley
For further information see: www.dkimages.com